MPOOK

Books should be returned or renewed by the last date above. Renew by phone **03000 41 31 31** or online *www.kent.gov.uk/libs*

D0420073

by the same author

Made for Good Purpose
What Every Parent Needs to Know to Help Their
Adolescent with Asperger's, High Functioning Autism or a
Learning Difference Become an Independent Adult
Michael P. McManmon
Foreword by Stephen M. Shore
ISBN 978 1 84905 863 6
eISBN 978 0 85700 435 2

Autism and Learning Differences
An Active Learning Teaching Toolkit
Michael P. McManmon
Foreword by Stephen M. Shore
ISBN 978 1 84905 794 3
eISBN 978 1 78450 074 0

of related interest

The Wonderful World of Work
A Workbook for Asperteens
Jeanette Purkis
Illustrated by Andrew Hore
ISBN 978 1 84905 499 7
eISBN 978 0 85700 923 4

Turning Skills and Strengths into Careers for Young
Adults with Autism Spectrum Disorder
The BASICS College Curriculum
Michelle Rigler, Amy Rutherford and Emily Quinn
ISBN 978 1 84905 798 1
eISBN 978 1 78450 096 2

Developing Identity, Strengths, and Self-Perception for
Young Adults with Autism Spectrum Disorder
The BASICS College Curriculum
Michelle Rigler, Amy Rutherford and Emily Quinn
ISBN 978 1 84905 797 4
eISBN 978 1 78450 095 5

MPLOY—A JOB READINESS WORKBOOK

CAREER SKILLS DEVELOPMENT FOR YOUNG ADULTS ON THE AUTISM SPECTRUM AND WITH LEARNING DIFFICULTIES

Michael P. McManmon with
Jenifer Kolarik and Michele Ramsay

Foreword by Carol Gray

Jessica Kingsley *Publishers*
London and Philadelphia

First published in 2018
by Jessica Kingsley Publishers
73 Collier Street
London N1 9BE, UK
and
400 Market Street, Suite 400
Philadelphia, PA 19106, USA

www.jkp.com

Copyright © Michael P. McManmon 2018
Foreword copyright © Carol Gray 2018

Library of Congress Cataloging in Publication Data
A CIP catalog record for this book is available from the Library of Congress

British Library Cataloguing in Publication Data
A CIP catalogue record for this book is available from the British Library

ISBN 978 1 78592 730 0
eISBN 978 1 78450 408 3

Printed and bound in the United States

Contents

PART III. THE EMPLOYMENT TOOLKIT

Foreword

I have had the opportunity to write several forewords. Never, though, has my work on behalf of people with autism so directly prepared me for providing testimony to the value and critical importance of a new book as it does with this one. If there's any advantage to being older, it is how our perspective broadens with each year. It makes us better consumers in the search for best practice in our field; the goals that are important and the methods that will best help us get there. Instead of wondering if a program or strategy will work, we recognize those that will. As a result of my experiences as a professional—and as someone who has known the lead author of this book, Dr. Michael McManmon, for many years—I believe that MPLOY: A Job Readiness Workbook is destined to be the unequalled "go to" resource for young people with autism and other learning difficulties, and those working on their behalf, as they navigate the bridge from education to employment.

I began my career as a teacher with four students with autism. On my desk was a framed note to myself: "These are not my children, and I cannot be with them in the future." Little did I know that I would be with them longer than I expected. I worked on their behalf for fifteen consecutive years. Of course, many other students joined my caseload along the way. The note on my desk was always there; a continual reminder to teach for the day when I would not be with them.

Several years into my teaching career, my position changed. I became a consultant, supporting those who worked directly with my students: parents, professionals, and (a new group of people to our program) owners and employees of businesses in our community. A federal grant made it possible for us to establish on-site vocational and career experiences for our students. It quickly became apparent where our past educational efforts were relevant, and also where we had wasted valuable time. There were concepts and skills that we had missed and needed to teach now. We revamped our curriculum to reflect what we were learning from the community and the world of work.

Most of our students graduated from our program into employment. On occasion to this day, I encounter them, usually where they have worked for years—and sometimes in their new place of work. My first year of teaching, I did have a sense that the future was closer than it seemed. What I didn't realize, though, was how very long the future is and how much we can accomplish there. I have watched yesterday's decisions "play out" today. One open door often leads to another for decades to come.

In the early 1990s, my students, our educational team, and the staff of our vocational training sites in the community had to navigate the trail between school and work without a compass. In sharp contrast, this workbook is on task, steadfastly focused, with no wasted time and a sense of what is needed to be ready for what lies ahead. It is an insightfully and intelligently paved road created by people who are amply qualified for the task.

I have known Dr. Michael McManmon, the lead author, for many years. I cannot remember exactly where we met. It is likely that our paths first crossed at a conference or workshop. Over the years, I have come to know Michael as a respected professional and a valued friend to reconnect with on the road. Michael was 53 years of age when he received the diagnosis with Asperger's Syndrome. His first-hand perspective growing up with autism, coupled with his education and professional experience, has led to an impressive list of contributions to our field. Wherever and whenever I have the opportunity to connect with Michael on the road, it is always a comfortable conversation with room to review, rethink, recharge…before we both move on to what life holds next. That's the Michael that isn't mentioned in his "Author's Note," but is evident throughout this volume. Michael has a rare talent. He casually and patiently helps others identify their path for what's ahead. Dr. Michael McManmon and his co-authors are more than qualified to guide you on the bridge from today to the future.

Regardless of what has brought you to consider this workbook, I've several years of trial, error, and experience to suggest that you have made a very smart choice. As I read the discussions in this workbook, reviewed the many case examples, and considered the practice activities, I was so impressed by the thought, insight, organization, and expertise behind them. I nodded as I recognized this workbook's value and its potential for success.

If you are a parent or professional working with young adults as they make the transition from school to work, this book will support you with a wealth of background information and hands-on ideas for practice. The same goes if you are a young adult making this transition on your own (or better yet with someone like a job coach or parent working with you). By selecting this workbook, you've completed the first step to a fulfilling future...very successfully. I join Michael and his co-authors with best wishes for the future. It begins on the following pages.

Carol Gray

Author's Note

You might not want to know this, but your real handicap may be the way you think about yourself. Otherwise, how do you explain individuals born without legs competing in the Olympics, or deaf individuals writing musical scores, or me founding five programs around the U.S. for young adults with Learning Differences and Autism Spectrum Disorder (ASD) after being diagnosed at the age of 53 with Asperger's?

Our own attitudes hold us back. Half the battle is simply learning to become *self-change agents*. The other half is following advice and being willing to change. It seems simplistic and it is. The problem is our own cognitive rigidity: we want to do the same things over and over, even though deep down we know that we aren't going to go anywhere without doing something different.

This workbook was designed specifically for young adults with Learning Differences and ASD. It will help you to make those attitude adjustments, find a career that matches your interests and abilities, and develop your practical skills. It is informed by my experience over the last 45 years working with students with Learning Differences. For most of that time I have operated my own group homes and programs, including the College Internship Program (CIP), a comprehensive training program that assists young adults on the Autism Spectrum and with Learning Differences to pursue employment, college degrees, and independent living. All of our students have gone on to find employment—in government agencies, hospitals, historical societies, gardens, markets, libraries, children's centers, the Coast Guard, technological institutions, and more—and they have attended colleges from the University of California to the Florida Institute of Technology.

While working with students on the Autism Spectrum, I earned a Masters in Counseling, a Masters in Human Development, and a Doctorate in Special Education and became a Licensed Psychologist—but I didn't start there. I was born into a family with seven brothers and sisters with many Learning Differences. My mom got me my first summer job in high school working at the church doing landscaping and painting. I was a shy, non-assertive boy who was very responsible but had no experience in the world of work. My struggles were the same as many of our students. I did not know what I wanted to do for work, but I had some special interests in gardening and art, and so my mom picked those areas to find jobs for me.

I was undiagnosed and pretty clueless about socialization, but I could talk to older adults on their level as they were interesting and had real knowledge of the world. I was hired by several of the neighbors to improve the landscape of their houses because

I worked hard and was inexpensive. I was very precise, enjoyed the work, and took my time doing the projects, and I had an artistic flare for arranging the plants and making the raised beds stand out (it is no accident that I have owned an organic farm for the last five years).

I took all of these experiences into account as I designed the programs and this workbook. Our fundamental philosophy is that students need to learn by doing and experiencing. From the beginning I was eclectic, using whatever was effective, knowing that it had to work both inside and outside the classroom. Today, we use community service, internships, and practicums as much as we do classroom and academic work. As with CIP, our emphasis in this workbook is for you to become your own self-change agent. We are only facilitators to set up the learning opportunities for you, the student. Like your parents, we help teach you and then release you into the wild!

This book is highly structured and will be easy for you to use. First, we have you develop an important understanding of yourself—who you are, what you need to thrive in the world of work—and help you find the best employer match. Then we describe the skills that employers need from you and how to develop them. Finally, we help you build your career portfolio, résumé, and cover letter, as well as develop interview skills.

Like most everything in life, just getting started is often the hardest part. Any experiences (even negative experiences) that help you to understand more about how to perform in your career area are going to give you invaluable knowledge and understanding to start building a career. You may need to start on a job doing menial tasks and work your way up to your dream job. Even volunteering for a company or business that you are interested in gets your foot in the door, and when you are in that environment you can learn a whole lot by just watching the operations. Always remember that *all work has dignity*, no matter whether you are emptying the trash or are the president of the corporation. Just starting somewhere is moving forward and building a career.

Sincerely,

Michael P. McManmon, Ed.D.

Why Seek Employment?

ALL WORK HAS DIGNITY

Finding employment is about more than an hourly wage (though of course income is nice, and the ultimate goal). Rationales for employment also include benefits, intellectual stimulation, socialization, career progression, building skills, contribution to society, and, most importantly, building self-esteem.

- *Income:* Although you may start your career by volunteering or with an unpaid internship, the long-term goal is to earn a living wage. This means you will be able to support yourself financially by paying rent and utilities, purchasing food, household items, and other goods and services, as well as treating yourself once in a while. Financial independence is truly liberating. You will have your own money and, with careful planning, be able to spend it according to the lifestyle you desire.

- *Benefits:* Some of the perks to being employed that we often don't think about are the insurance and retirement benefits that come along with it. For most of the population, if you are unemployed and you get sick or need to go to the dentist, or if you or your spouse want to have a baby, the bills will be totally unaffordable—unless you have health insurance. Insurance itself can also be expensive, but if you are employed, your employer takes just a little bit of money out of your check each month and then covers all of your (and often your partner's) medical bills. If you are injured or sick, your employer will probably still pay your salary until you can come back to work. Finally, many employers will also help you set up a retirement fund so that when you are old and no longer able to work, you will have some money to live on.

- *Intellectual stimulation:* Whatever its other comforts, staying at home is boring. As human beings, we crave learning and stimulation, and when we don't get these things, we can feel depressed and unfulfilled. But when we embark on a career search, learn new skills, and interact with new people, the neurons in our brains are like fireworks. Learning any new skill is a deep, fulfilling joy and pleasure, and as you work your way through the career continuum, your cognitive abilities and horizons will continue expanding.

- *Socialization:* In the same way we need intellectual stimulation, human beings are social animals who need social interaction. But it can be hard sometimes to get out there and meet new people. Like exercise, socializing is an action we sometimes force ourselves to do, and then feel great about afterwards when we're finished. Having a job will allow you to interact with others in a controlled, comfortable environment. At the same time, you will build your socialization skills as you practice them every day at work.

- *Career progression:* Although you may not want to embark on a career search knowing that you may have to start by making little or no money, you must keep in mind that one position leads to the next. If you work hard, you will advance. Along the way, though your pay may be low, you will be compensated through experience, building skills, networking, and making the connections that can lead to better-paid positions down the road.

- *Building skills:* You never know what kinds of skills you're going to learn on the job, and no matter your position, you will learn something new, whether it's how to talk to co-workers, follow directions, organize a room, take charge, or build something with your hands. You can take the skills you build with you as you advance to better and better positions.

- *Contribution to society:* We live in a world in which we all rely on everyone to do their job so that society can function. You use the Internet or do your work on computers that were developed by engineers who conducted research at public universities. You live in houses and work in buildings built by construction workers who were educated in trade schools. Those who can't earn a living because of disabilities or because they are at home taking care of children rely on government and volunteer services for help. When you join the workforce, you join in this great machinery that allows communities to flourish and society to function. In addition, part of your income will go to taxes that pay for the roads, schools, libraries, and other public works we all rely on.

- *Building self-esteem:* The confidence you will build on the job is priceless. Working to solve problems at work, earning a living, learning new skills, advancing through the career continuum to better positions, and seeing yourself as a part of a team and a contributing member of your community are actions that will boost your self-esteem in inestimable ways.

How to Use This Book

This workbook is intended for young adults with Learning Differences and Autism Spectrum Disorder (ASD) who are trying to decide on the best career choice. It will help you navigate your special interests and ability areas to learn what kind of career you may want to pursue. It will teach you the eight skills employers look for; help you build your career portfolio, résumés, cover letters, and interview skills; and prepare you for life on the job. Although you can work your way through the book alone, the best way to do it is with a *job coach*: a teacher, parent, career coordinator, or other counselor who can help you navigate the complexities of preparing for a job search.

CONTENT OUTLINE

In *Part I* of this book we guide you through the process of developing your special interests and ability areas. Part I will help you discover which abilities you need to develop in order to perform the jobs you are interested in, and it also teaches you how to develop realistic ideas about the jobs you can perform. For example, you may have a high interest in being a sports announcer but little ability in public speaking, so you have to either develop the necessary public speaking skills or find a job in the same field which you do have the ability to perform.

Part I is broken into three chapters. First, we describe the Career Continuum: how you can work your way from volunteering to internships to full employment. Second, we help you explore various career choices and provide exercises for determining your skills and interests. Finally, we provide several worksheets to help you discover which kinds of jobs would be most fitting for you, according to your employer, environmental, sensory, social, intellectual, and emotional fit.

In *Part II* we describe the eight main skills that employers are looking for: Communication, Teamwork, Problem Solving and Critical Thinking, Initiative and Leadership, Planning and Organizing, Self-Management, Willingness to Learn, and Technological Proficiency. People like me sometimes think they're proficient in these skills because they have strong minds and good memories, but in fact they don't know how to use the skills effectively in real life. I always say that I could write a great book on relationships, but trying to be in a relationship is often a disaster for me. So in this section, we give stories and practical advice about how to develop and work on these skills. If you can learn and master them, then you are guaranteed success.

Finally, in *Part III*, we provide a toolkit to help you create a career portfolio, résumé, cover letter, and sample job applications: exercises to help you prepare for job interviews; and practical advice for when you land the position you've been seeking.

In each part, we concentrate on real-life, transferable skills that have been proven to be effective. We present this material to you in several formats to enable you to absorb as much information as painlessly as possible, including exercises, tips, and real stories about our students at CIP to illustrate important points. If you take the time to complete all of the worksheets, learn and begin practicing the eight skills we've outlined, and build your career portfolio, résumé, and interview skills, then you will be on your way toward finding a fruitful and satisfying career.

PART I
Developing Your Interests and Ability Areas

CHAPTER ONE

The Career Continuum

Continuum of Employment

Each skill we acquire has a starting point and develops over time. Jobs and employment are the same. As we build our skills we move towards more advanced jobs and usually higher pay. The ultimate goal of the Career Continuum is for you to leverage your passion into pay—find out what your interests are through volunteering and internships, and work towards finding a paid position in that area—but you have to start somewhere, and anywhere is fine.

Sometimes we develop a skill or desire to work after doing community service. Internships or apprenticeships are another great way for employers to get low-cost help and also provide training and education to students. These are win-win situations. You can gain transferable skills at the same time as helping others or gaining college credit. All of your experiences will increase your knowledge and value as a potential employee, as well as help you to develop and hone your own interests.

LEVERAGE YOUR PASSION INTO PAY

STORY

Being willing to learn and grow is the most important attitude we need to bring to our work. Those who went through the great depression appreciated any work they could get. My dad started as a stock boy in a Montgomery Ward Department Store in Chicago and shortly afterwards my mom gave birth to the first of my parents' nine children. Dad started by doing menial labor and slowly moved up to ordering and assisting the buyers. After about ten years, he was promoted to work in the National Office in New York City as a buyer in the boys' clothing department.

There is a saying: if everyone who was going to have a baby waited until they were married, and both parents had great jobs, owned a house, and had money in the bank, the population of the world would be zero. No one feels that their lives are perfect, and everyone is working towards some higher goal. It's the journey that counts. Any experience on any job is worthwhile. Do not minimize the experience you are obtaining! We learn a lot of transferable skills on any job—for example, how to fill out a timecard, get along with co-workers, deal with customers, or follow directions.

My dad is proud of what he was able to accomplish with a high school education, and he made sure that all of us had a college education so we could go even farther.

1. COMMUNITY SERVICE / VOLUNTEERING

My motto is that *community service introduces you to yourself.* By giving to others, you learn a lot about who you are and who you want to be. Community service is also a great way to understand what skills you have and what areas of work you might enjoy. It is an easy way to get experience and help others at the same time. You can learn organizational skills by learning how to organize the food at a food bank or volunteering to set up for a community dinner. Whether you are cleaning a restroom at a homeless shelter or delivering meals to the elderly, remember: *All work has dignity.*

COMMUNITY SERVICE INTRODUCES YOU TO YOURSELF

STORY

We had a student, April, who was partially blind and had some other physical ailments that affected her mobility. She volunteered for every community service opportunity that was available at the center. She even provided leadership in developing some herself, including a Walk for Hunger and a Thanksgiving Food Drive. She was always trying to do something for others despite her own disabilities. Her attitude was exemplary, which made her a role model to her peers.

April had an aneurism in her brain and died unexpectedly. Her picture and a poem that she wrote are framed on the wall at our center in Massachusetts, and we planted a flowering cherry tree with a plaque in front of it at the center. She will always be remembered for her love of helping others less fortunate than herself.

"During my time here at the center, I was able to accomplish quite a few things. I participated in the walk for the homeless. I can proudly say I walked three miles. I was also able to organize a clothing drive for the needy. I've been able to collect a lot of clothing. That in itself is a success. I also visited seniors. A lot of enjoyment can be gained in helping others."

April Beattie Farrell

2. SUPERVISED INTERNSHIP

Having a supervised internship with a job coach or counselor is another way to get more specific experience in a job area that you think you might be interested in. You could also *job shadow* an employee on their job for a day or more to see if that type of work is what you enjoy or would be a good fit for you.

Many jobs and graduate programs even require applicants to complete internships before applying. For example, most veterinary schools and law schools require that prospective students have real experience working or interning in veterinary clinics or legal offices before applying. This is required because many students don't want to practice after graduation due to the lack of experience and understanding of the realities of the job. The schools don't want to waste spots in their programs on students who won't stay in the field.

STORY

I remember when Sally first interviewed for CIP and we discussed her career goals. She replied that since she was a child she always knew she wanted to work with animals and possibly even go to school one day to become a veterinarian. When asked if she had a "Plan B," she quickly replied NO. She absolutely loved animals, cats in particular, and she was confident that a career with animals was all she wanted.

In Sally's first term at CIP, she was accepted at two internships that worked with animals, one

being the zoo and the other being the humane society. At the humane society, Sally refused to work with the dogs and only wanted to sit in a room and pet cats. At the zoo, Sally was very limited in the areas that she was willing to intern because she did not realize how much the different odors from the various animals would negatively affect her senses. Sally discovered that, in fact, she did not want to pursue a career as a veterinarian.

Having the opportunity to volunteer or intern in a career choice of interest is essential in identifying "the right fit." Had Sally started college classes to become a veterinarian, she may have taken years of education in the wrong classes and wasted financial funding in an area that was not the right intellectual fit.

—Michele Ramsay, Program Director, CIP Brevard

3. INTERNSHIP TO WORK

Many times your skill set may be underdeveloped for the job that you are seeking. You may need a long internship to learn all the small skills necessary for the employer to be willing to pay you a salary. Start with an unpaid internship and then, with both your job coach and employer, determine which skills you would need to learn in order to gain a paying position. The job coach may be able to negotiate with the employer to extend this internship so that they can work on these areas, with a view to employment at a future set date.

STORY

Natalie was a second-year student at the Massachusetts Center. She spent one day a week during her first year volunteering at a community dinner and helping out in a food pantry at a local church. Doing this helped Natalie in so many ways. She learned some valuable pre-employment skills as well as being able to acquire "customer service" skills as she served the older people who attended the weekly event dinners or the less fortunate members of the community who came to the food bank. Natalie really liked meeting and greeting people, and helping them.

Natalie told her career coordinator that she wanted to work as a cashier at a local drug store and her coordinator was able to secure an internship for Natalie. For her initial internship assignment, Natalie was taught how to do the "store inventory" and she became responsible for it.

A career coordinator offers students realistic career counseling and advice. This includes the fact that once on the job or internship our students may very well have to "start at the bottom," doing the "grunt work" to prove they are capable; and have to work hard to show they have further ability. Our students soon realize that by doing this they will gain experience, become part of a team, and earn the respect from supervisors and co-workers that will lead to building a solid foundation for advancement.

In Natalie's case, she did well during her probationary period. Because of this, her career coordinator was able to approach Natalie's manager and set up an internship-to-work agreement. Natalie would continue her internship at the store for three additional months and during that time she would be trained in the operation of the cash register. If all went well, then Natalie would be hired as a cashier. This is a good example of a successful internship. Natalie gave the employer three months of "free help," and the employer gave Natalie a chance to pursue a career that would allow her to do the customer service work she coveted. Natalie successfully completed the additional three months required by the internship-to-work agreement and was hired as a paid employee.

4. EMPLOYMENT

Working a job for pay is very rewarding, and it's the ultimate goal. To become employed, you may have to start part-time to get your foot in the door, or take a position that is not exactly the one you want. Your first job may not have all the benefits and salary that you desire, but if you do a good job, it will provide you with a valuable reference if and when another opportunity for advancement comes your way.

STORY

Many students have exaggerated aspirations regarding salary and status in the workplace. I asked a student named Paul how much salary he would like to make at a job. He said one million dollars per year (working as little as possible of course)! The concept of just getting one's foot in the door, starting at the bottom and working your way up, is foreign to many of our students. Even students who just received their college degree struggle to get their foot in the door! So teaching them that "you have to start somewhere" and work your way up is critical.

Another student, Susan, who has her college degree, had been interning for a local library for over a year and had received excellent reviews. When she started to apply for jobs within the library system, she was offered interview after interview without receiving a job offer. After 10 months and 11 interviews, she was finally offered a job—but it was only a temp job for a library that needed help but didn't have a permanent position. She took it anyway because she knew it would give her the edge she needed to advance to a permanent library job.

Within one month, Susan had another interview and was offered a permanent position. She then kept her eye out for better-paying jobs within the local libraries, and about a year later she was able to move into a position with significantly higher pay. Given her degree, her experience, and her abilities, Susan is now positioned to continually advance within the library system— but it took a lot of initial perseverance and someone willing to "give her a break" to make it all happen!

—*Jennifer Kolarik, Career Coordinator, CIP Brevard*

CHAPTER TWO

Exploring Career Choices

Before you begin a career search, you must gather as much information as possible about yourself (your interests, the skills you have, and the skills you need to obtain) as well as the possible career paths related to your interests and the skills necessary to follow those paths. In this chapter you will learn how to build a relationship with your job coach, take stock of and build up your transferable skills, and decide what your greatest interests are and which career choices would match your skills and interests.

Explaining Career Choices

1. BUILD A RELATIONSHIP WITH YOUR JOB COACH

The best way to work through this book is with a job coach. A job coach acts as a guide through your career search, a support person while you're on the job, and a liaison between you and employers or potential employers. They will help you set up volunteer work, internships, and/or paid employment. When you begin working, you will meet with your job coach periodically to discuss your trials, successes, and general experience at work. Your job coach may also communicate with your employer about your progress. The goal is for you to build your workability and other skills so that eventually you can search for better jobs and remain employed independently, without their help.

HOW TO FIND A JOB COACH

If you are enrolled in an educational or other kind of program, there may be specific staff members on site to act as job coaches. If not, talk to your advisor or counselor about who the appropriate person would be. If you're not enrolled in a program, think of someone you trust—perhaps a teacher, mentor, or parent—and consider asking them to act as your job coach. Remember, being open and willing to ask for help is an important part of your career search.

THINGS TO KEEP IN MIND

1. The first thing you must do is to build rapport, trust, and workability with your job coach. This is equally as important as the knowledge you hope to obtain during your time working with them. Creating an atmosphere of trust and unconditional acceptance is necessary to start the process. Later on in the process, you may be open enough to accept corrective criticism to assist in your growth.

2. Discuss your interests with your job coach, including what areas you currently enjoy and those you want to learn more about. Be open and honest with your job coach about your hopes, fears, and abilities.

3. Work with your job coach as part of a team that includes your employer or internship supervisors, school advisors, career counselors, teachers, and parents.

4. Give feedback to your job coach about what they could do to make your internship or job a positive, enriching experience.

5. Listen carefully to the constructive feedback your job coach gives you. Remember that they are on your team, and that they want you to be successful. Try to make the changes they suggest. Be willing and open to trying new things.

6. Remember that finding a career is a process. You may not be satisfied on your first volunteering position, internship, or even paid position. Work with your job coach to advance through the Career Continuum.

7. Finally, keep in mind that the ultimate goal is to eventually be capable of working independently, without the help of a job coach. Time spent with your job coach should build your independence and confidence to work alone.

STORY

A good example of this process occurred at Bradley Farm last year. Aaron, a CIP Berkshire student, was interested in being a deliveryman, possibly for FedEx or UPS. He was open and willing to do delivery services locally first, with some possibilities for growth down the road. Aaron began interning at Bradley Farm, where he tended to animals, planted and harvested vegetables and fruits, and stocked the farm store shelves when a delivery came in. He would also deliver some of the harvest to a local farm-to-table restaurant and organize it on their shelves.

As a job coach I began to ask Aaron what areas he enjoyed and what areas he wanted to learn about. I talked with his advisors, his career counselor, his teachers, and his parents when they visited. I would continually ask for his feedback and what I could add or change in his internship to make his experience the best possible for him. He shared his love of delivery and how important it made him feel to help others.

Over several months I watched this student grow, increasing his skills, techniques, confidence, and self-esteem. Starting with his interest in delivery services, Aaron was able to branch out and work with me to try new things way out of his comfort zone, discuss his feelings and thoughts, and accept constructive feedback. Eventually he was hired in a paid position at Bradley Farm. He was motivated to get his driver's license, purchase a car with his parents' assistance, and become a full-time employee of the farm store over the summer months.

With the help and support of his job coach using neutral to positive statements, Aaron not only became a successful paid employee at his internship, but he also went on to be hired at a local health food store in the stock room, and he now works independently without the use of a job coach or support services. He is very proud of his success and hopes to continue to work in the field of stock and delivery for many years to come.

—*Brenda Brown, MSW, Career Counselor and Job Coach, CIP Berkshire*

2. BUILD TRANSFERABLE SKILLS

Spend time on real-life skills that will help you gain and keep employment. Transferable skills are skills that most people can use on just about any job, such as being on time, calling in if you are sick, taking only the amount of time on breaks that you are entitled to, or dressing appropriately for the job. They also include the eight skills employers look for (described in Part II of this workbook). You can already begin building your transferable skills while working in your current position. You can also learn these skills on almost any community service or internship site, and they will directly apply to a paid employment opportunity.

STORY

Dan wanted to be a graphic designer. While he was searching for a position, he decided to take temporary, part-time work on evenings and weekends as residential assistant working with young adults with Learning Differences. Dan listened well to the students and treated them with honesty and integrity. They were drawn to his quiet confidence. The company needed someone to assist in developing their website and Dan took on some additional hours to do that. His networking skills, resourcefulness, and creativity became apparent and he was offered a full-time position working with IT and the students. Dan's transferable communication, teamwork, and leadership allowed him to advance to a position he wanted to have.

You can use these working at a sanitation plant or on Wall Street.

HARD SKILLS VS. SOFT SKILLS

So far we've primarily discussed building hard skills: teachable abilities that are easy to quantify, such as computer operation, writing, getting your driver's license, earning a certificate, or phone courtesy.

Employers, however, are also looking for soft skills, sometimes described as "people skills" or "interpersonal skills," which are more nebulous and harder to measure. Soft skills relate to the way you interact with others, and include flexibility, patience, empathy, creativity, time management, communication, teamwork, and motivation.

Any particular job position will require a few specific hard skills—but almost every job will require those soft, people skills. Employers need motivated, understanding employees, and they will look for those soft skills on your résumé. Although it is easy for an employer to train an employee in a certain hard skill, soft skills are much harder to teach, and employers want applicants who already have them. We'll address some of these skills in more detail in Part II: Eight Skills Employers Look For.

EXERCISE

TRANSFERABLE SKILLS WORKSHEET

Complete an inventory of your transferable skills, and then fill out the **Transferable Skills Summary and Action Plan** from this information. **Place a check next to the skills you possess. Circle or underline skills you would like to acquire.**

SENSITIVITY TO OTHERS:

- ☐ Able to maintain a deep interest in the concerns and feelings of others.
- ☐ Inclined to find ways to help people.
- ☐ Able to tolerate the actions of others.

INSIGHT INTO OTHERS:

- ☐ Have an understanding of what makes people do what they do.
- ☐ Tolerant of the actions of others.
- ☐ Good at reading the moods of others.

OPENNESS:

- ☐ Able to encourage communication with all people at many different levels.
- ☐ Inclined to share personal experiences and trust people.

RESPECT:

- ☐ Able to take the feelings, needs, thoughts, wishes, and preferences of others (including other cultures and races) into consideration, and give them worth and value.
- ☐ Able to give work and value to others' ideas.

SPEAKING:

- ☐ Able to introduce yourself.
- ☐ Able to present information clearly and confidently to other individuals and groups.
- ☐ Can maintain good eye contact and can keep the attention of an audience or individual.

Transferable Skills Worksheet continues

ACTIVE LISTENING:

☐ Able to devote full attention to what other people are saying and listen without interrupting.

☐ Can take the time to understand the points being made and ask clarifying questions as needed, and do not interrupt inappropriately.

COMMUNICATION:

☐ Able to speak clearly.

☐ Able to read body language and use appropriate body language.

☐ Able to hold a reciprocal conversation.

PERSUASION AND LEADERSHIP:

☐ Able to influence people, their beliefs, and actions.

☐ Able to win cooperation and support for ideas or activities from others.

☐ Have the ability to communicate a vision or goal to others and lead them towards achieving it.

☐ Can push for action results and win the support and help of others.

TEAMWORK:

☐ Able to work easily with a group of people and show loyalty and commitment to the team's objectives.

☐ Able to accept each member's viewpoint equally.

☐ Able to openly express views and opinions within a group.

☐ Can demonstrate willingness to take on tasks and responsibilities.

PLANNING:

☐ Can create clear goals and identify and find the resources (e.g., time, people, materials) needed to achieve them.

☐ Able to schedule tasks so that work is completed on time.

TIME MANAGEMENT:

☐ Able to organize events and tasks carefully so as to use time efficiently.

☐ Can use calendar/planner to plan ahead and make sure deadlines are met.

Transferable Skills Worksheet continues

GOAL SETTING AND INITIATIVE:

☐ Able to make a decision about what is needed or wanted and able to determine when it is to be achieved.

☐ Can stay on task, stay committed to a goal, and deal with setbacks realistically.

☐ Able to take steps to improve a situation.

☐ Able to seek opportunities to influence events or make decisions.

☐ Able to perform tasks independently or with minimum support or direction.

COMPUTING:

☐ Can confidently use a computer to write documents, browse the internet, and use email programs.

☐ Can save files, locate them efficiently, and print them.

PROBLEM SOLVING:

☐ Able to seek answers and find the cause of problems.

☐ Can choose effective solutions and take the necessary action to resolve them.

LEARNING:

☐ Able to seek new opportunities to learn.

☐ Able to demonstrate an interest in learning new things and in personal development.

☐ Able to seek feedback to improve understanding.

ADAPTABILITY:

☐ Able to adapt easily to new challenges and remain open to new ways of doing things.

☐ Able to change or rearrange plans or actions to deal with evolving situations.

TOOLS AND TECHNOLOGY:

☐ Able to use equipment, tools, or technology effectively.

☐ Can follow instructions and show willingness to use whatever tools or technology is required.

Transferable Skills Worksheet continues

MOTIVATION:

☐ Can exhibit the drive (or determination) to succeed and excel at tasks.

☐ Able to exceed expectations.

☐ Able to show confidence in abilities and expect to succeed at all tasks agreed upon.

DEPENDABILITY:

☐ Can demonstrate reliability and responsibility in fulfilling duties.

☐ Can carefully check all work to ensure all details have been considered.

PROFESSIONALISM:

☐ Able to remain calm and self-controlled in stressful situations.

☐ Able to stay focused and to deliver the best interests of the organization at all times.

☐ Able to exhibit good hygiene and maintain an appropriate dress code.

☐ Able to keep desk and work area clean and organized.

☐ Can carefully check all work to ensure all details have been considered.

EXERCISE

TRANSFERABLE SKILLS SUMMARY AND ACTION PLAN

Now that you are familiar with some of the most important transferable skills desired by employers, it is a good idea to make a list of those you have developed the most. These will be some of the things you would mention when writing your résumé, along with some examples of how they were developed or used.

You can also use this information when preparing for a job interview. An employer will be looking to see what skills you have and for evidence of how you have actually applied them.

Most employers want just about all of the skills mentioned on the Transferable Skills Worksheet. So why not set targets for developing some of your weaker skills?

Start by listing some of the skills you would like to get more experience in and then note some of the activities you could become involved in to help develop them.

MY MOST DEVELOPED SKILLS

Skill name	How you developed it	How you use it
1.		
2.		
3.		
4.		
5.		
6.		
7.		
8.		

Transferable Skills Summary and Action Plan continues

SKILLS I NEED OR WANT TO DEVELOP

Skill name	Way/activity to develop it	Desired training
1.		
2.		
3.		
4.		
5.		
6.		
7.		
8.		

3. DISCOVER CAREER INTERESTS

Follow the yellow brick road! What are you interested in? What are you excited about sharing and developing? Look first for clues in those areas. It is important to note that just because someone has a deep interest or knowledge in a certain area, it does not mean they have the ability to operate as an employee in that area.

STORY

Chris was a student who memorized all the stats and information about each player on the Boston Red Socks baseball team. He desperately wanted to become a sports announcer. He was very shy and socially awkward, though, and did not have the verbal skills to communicate with roommates or teachers.

Chris worked with his job coach and she laid out a plan to assist him in developing the communication skills he would need to obtain employment in this area. In this case, he did not have the motivation to try to learn the verbal skills necessary to do this job, so they needed to look for other related areas he could work in, or choose another field of his special interests as a career choice. Chris needed pre-employment internships to show him the skill areas that he excelled in, as well as the ones he lacked skills in, but he was rigid in his thinking and wanted only to be an announcer. He did not want to attempt any internship.

Chris did have a good heart and wanted to help others, so his job coach set him up in a community service position that would enable him to work with disabled children playing sports. Chris really enjoyed this and was motivated to go to his community service every time it was on his schedule. He slowly started to communicate more in this safe environment and was able to listen to advice and start to follow suggestions. He became motivated to accept help with his reciprocal conversation and self-advocacy skills.

It took Chris a year to build enough confidence and self-esteem to be able to start an internship assisting a physical therapist at a children's clinic. After he did this successfully, he had the desire to start taking classes to become a Physical Therapy Aide, and he is now gainfully employed.

Chris's story shows how it is a slow process—sometimes over years—to come to realistic conclusions about yourself on your own. As teachers and job coaches we want to respect the process and your rights to make your own decisions while at the same time create a safe place for you to start to experiment. Firm guidance can assist in the process. You need to come to a point where you see for yourself that accepting help is a good thing.

Everyone has "islands of competency": special skills that are unique to a small set of people. As you uncover these unique skills you will have some clues regarding what employment direction you want to take.

EXERCISE

USE THE INTERNET TO DISCOVER CAREER INTERESTS

Utilize this list of career resource websites to determine personal interest areas and potential career choices:

- *The Princeton Review Career Quiz:* www.princetonreview.com/quiz/career-quiz

- *The O*Net Interest Profiler:* www.mynextmove.org/explore/ip

- *CareerOneStop Interest Assessment:* www.careeronestop.org/toolkit/careers/interest-assessment.aspx

- *The Career Interest Questionnaire:* www.wistechcolleges.org/explore-careers/career-interest-questionnaire

- *The Career Cluster Interest Survey:* www.careerwise.mnscu.edu/careers/clusterSurvey

- *The Motivational Appraisal of Personal Potential (MAPP):* www.assessment.com

CHAPTER THREE

Goodness of Fit

Once you have decided what interests you and what careers you're most interested in, you have to find a job with the "right fit." This is one of the most important skills for you to learn. Only you know what kind of people you want to be around and what type of environment you want to work in. Only you know what lighting and noise you can tolerate.

In order to set yourself up for success, you need to honor your emotional, social, and sensory needs and not waste time looking at employment in places that you know you will be anxious or unhappy. As we say at CIP, the structure supports your growth. When you find the right employment structure, you will flourish. In this chapter we will help you discover the best fit.

1. EMPLOYER FIT

Do you like to be around creative people? Quiet people? Would you prefer a supervisor who was friendly and casual or one who was more business-like? Matching yourself to the right type of employer is similar to matching yourself to a friend or a partner. Even though you won't have the intimacy that you would with a girlfriend or boyfriend, you do have to spend a large amount of time at work each day, and

it is important to be with people you feel trusting, comfortable, and relaxed with. Although we cannot always find the "perfect fit," and all relationships have conflict and can go sour, we still need to make a living and support ourselves, and this section will help you narrow down your choices to find the best fit possible.

STORY

Jeremiah liked to be around creative people. He was able to study and even write his college papers while listening to his music. He got along best with students who were extroverts and were very verbal, and he preferred to be around people who expressed themselves constantly.

Jeremiah was also interested in learning culinary skills. Taking this all into account, his job coach steered him toward a hip organic foods co-op café, where there were several employees like him already. Jeremiah loved working with these types of co-workers and was met with instant acceptance. He was able to work in the kitchen creating the food for the hot food bar and learn the culinary skills he desired.

EXERCISE

EMPLOYER FIT

Circle the top four attributes that you would prefer an employer to have. Circle the top four challenges that you would have with an employer at a job site.

Employer assets	Employer challenges
Good mentor	Micromanager
Pleasant personality	Aggressive or irritable
Female	Female
Male	Male
Highly educated	Low educational level
Non-aggressive	Assertive
Friendly	Unfriendly
Experienced	Poor communicator
Good teacher	Prefers you work on your own
Professional	Unprofessional
Good communicator	Quiet, doesn't say much
Workability	Rigid or uncompromising

2. ENVIRONMENTAL FIT

Do you need a window or natural light to feel calm? Or do you work best in an enclosed quiet space away from others? Does it make a difference to you if other workers are in close proximity to you? Or do you need to be off by yourself to work best? What type of environments do you flourish in? What type of environments cause you stress? Environmental fit refers to the actual physical structure of the employment site, both inside and out. An office complex a long bus ride from home may not be best for you, or a high-rise building downtown. You may not want to work in a large mall or in a dark neighborhood at night. Every individual has their own desires in this area. Some people move to the city from a farm in Kansas to work; others move from New York City to a farm in New Hampshire.

A NOTE ON PERSONAL SPACE

Individuals on the Autism Spectrum or with Learning Differences tend to require a little more personal space. This might include having your own office, cubicle, or other space that you can retreat to, or a certain number of breaks per day for you to be alone and gather yourself. When looking for a job, remember to think about how much personal space you need and whether the work environment will provide for it.

STORY

Lia was a quiet and reserved student who wanted to study library science. She was an excellent scholar and had no problem passing her courses. She needed an internship site to help her learn about what she might want to do after graduation.

Her career coordinator suggested several sites and they decided to visit a few to see what she might prefer. They visited a large university library, an elementary school library, and a public library in a small town. Lia chose the small public library for three reasons: 1) employer fit: the librarian she would work with was very reserved and pleasant, and she felt she could work with her well; 2) sensory fit: it was calm and quiet, especially compared to the university library, which was teeming with studying, gossiping undergraduates, and the elementary school library, which was filled with noisy children; and most importantly for Lia was 3) environmental fit: it was in a small community atmosphere and she would have her own cubicle where she could work quietly on her own for a few hours each day.

EXERCISE

ENVIRONMENTAL FIT CHECKLIST

List the "must have" aspects of environments you would like to work in. Then list your "can't stands." Prioritize them from 1 to 10, with 1 being the most important.

Must haves	Can't stands

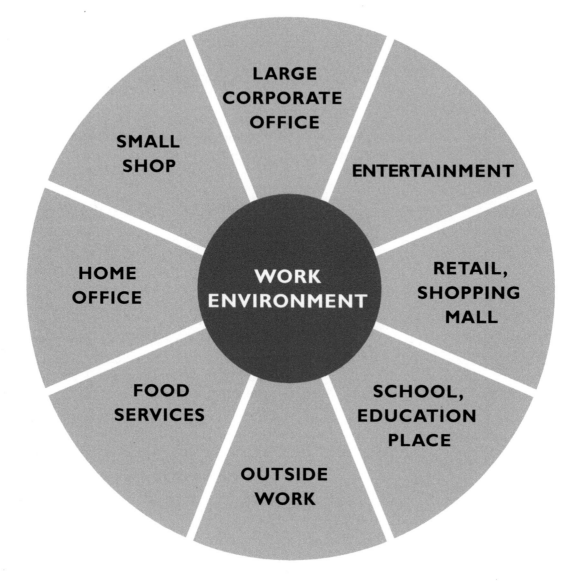

3. SENSORY FIT

Finding the right sensory match is vital to your comfort and wellness on the job.

Do you prefer bright lights or dim lights? Can you function with background music playing in the office? Or air conditioning and fans operating near you? Do certain scents or chemical odors offend you? You need to take all of these into account when you are searching for a job site or a career choice. For example, if you want to work with animals but you cannot stand the smell of their feces, then you need to either figure out how you can work with them without running into this issue, or choose another interest area.

STORY

Stephen had a lot of sensory issues. The most pronounced were his sensitivity to light, loud music, and noise. He wanted to work as an accountant and started to look for an internship with an accounting firm.

He looked at a large firm that had a whole floor of cubicles where the employees worked under bright fluorescent lights. He knew he would feel too disturbed by the noise, lack of privacy, and the lighting. He looked at another accounting firm that was located in a noisy neighborhood with a building under construction next door. He eliminated that one as well.

He then looked at a small family firm that was located in an older home turned into offices. This firm had only one or two employees in each room and had incandescent lighting and desk lamps. It was a comfortable environment with doors at each office to keep the noise down. Stephen applied for his internship at this company.

EXERCISE

SENSORY FIT CHECKLIST

List your sensory assets in the left column and your sensory challenges in the right column. Then prioritize them from 1 to 10, with 1 being the most important.

Sensory assets	Sensory challenges

4. SOCIAL FIT

Are you looking for a highly interactive job site where staff communicate often, work in teams, and rely on their communication skills to accomplish their jobs? Do you do better with older people, your peers, or younger people? Are you better off with one supervisor than a group of individuals dealing with you on the job? What are your social assets and deficit areas and how will they translate to this job or career?

STORY

We once worked with a student named David who had ADHD. He was very active, distractible, and not able to sit still for very long, which gave him trouble with his academic classes. Although his social skills were limited, David was very sociable and loved to talk to people, and he was good with short conversations.

After many attempts to place David in an internship, we found the perfect volunteer position at a hospital. He took a cart room-to-room and floor-to-floor to offer magazines and newspapers to the patients for them to read. He was very successful in navigating the entire hospital and getting to know all the staff, and had a positive disposition that made him well liked by the hospital staff. They looked forward to his happy greetings. He loved being busy and moving all the time.

This job provided David with a social and emotional outlet, and the ability to use his social skills. When a paid position delivering medical supplies on a cart around the hospital came open, the staff encouraged him to apply. He got that job and was very successful at it.

EXERCISE

SOCIAL FIT CHECKLIST

List your social assets in the left column and your social challenges in the right column. Then prioritize them from 1 to 10, with 1 being the most important.

Social assets	Social challenges

5. INTELLECTUAL FIT

Is the intellectual content of your work stimulating enough to keep your interest? Are the individuals around you on the job capable enough to stimulate your intellect? Is there a chance for upward mobility—moving up the chain of command towards more intellectual work after laboring at the bottom?

STORY

Jan's special interest was programming mobile applications, video games, and other software, but she had trouble finding a job in this competitive field. She found a job as a data entry clerk at a local medical laboratory, but she struggled with the boring nature of this work and thought it was below her abilities. It wasn't the right intellectual fit.

Jan was determined to work at the lab only to make a living, and in the meantime continue to hone her programming skills and apply for jobs that she felt would be intellectually stimulating. She continued her programming education by taking evening classes at the local state university, and signed up for weekend workshops. She networked with her classmates, professors, and other programmers online, and she finally got an interview for a position programming mobile apps for a sports entertainment company. She knew this would be a stimulating and challenging intellectual fit.

EXERCISE

INTELLECTUAL FIT CHECKLIST

List your intellectual assets in the left column and your intellectual challenges in the right column. Then prioritize them from 1 to 10, with 1 being the most important.

Intellectual assets	Intellectual challenges

6. EMOTIONAL FIT

Is this job going to contribute to your emotional wellbeing? How will you feel on this job? Does this job support your emotional growth or constrict you? What is your inner sense regarding this type of employment or this specific job you are applying for? Emotional fit is extremely important to consider when choosing a career for yourself.

STORY

Jarrod was a student from Pennsylvania who had attended a private learning disabilities boarding school in New York. He was well traveled and had the basic social skills in public. He was handsome and in good shape. At the same time, Jarrod was very intimidated and embarrassed when asked a question in front of anyone. He hid out quite often in his apartment and preferred to isolate himself rather than be out in public.

Jarrod really wanted to be employed and his basic work skills were good. He liked doing inventory and had a good memory for keeping track of things. After several internships at stores, he finally landed a position at Home Depot where he was a stock clerk. Within a couple of months, Jarrod knew where every item was in the store, what aisle, and how far down.

The problem was that Jarrod did not like to interact with customers. He was able to get and keep this position mostly because he had a kind, sympathetic, and understanding supervisor who was patient with him and took the time to explain things clearly to him. Jarrod slowly got more comfortable with tasks such as answering customers' questions and directing them to the right aisle. He was an asset to the store, as he knew where everything was, and was calm (at least on the outside). Unfortunately, Jarrod's supervisor left her job unexpectedly, and his new supervisor had little patience with Jarrod, expecting him to "just do what he said." Jarrod could not live up to this supervisor's expectations and soon was so uncomfortable that he quit the job.

After a long period of unemployment, Jarrod, with the help of his career coordinator, was able to muster the courage to get a job doing stock at a small hardware store closer to his apartment. Although his experience at the Home Depot ended negatively, the experience he gained there was the main reason he was hired. In addition, the family who owned the store had a cousin with developmental disabilities, and they understood how to be patient and kind with Jarrod.

A NOTE ON STRESS

Many individuals on the spectrum struggle with anxiety or depression and tend to shut down (or have a strong emotional reaction) when feeling stressed. Potential sources of stress in the workplace may include social interactions with your supervisor or co-workers, elevated sensory inputs (sounds, bright lights, etc.), the pressure to meet expectations or deadlines, performing certain tasks, having to multi-task, or annual evaluations.

While it is difficult to foresee how stressful interactions might be with a supervisor or co-workers, you can partially evaluate how stressful a job might be based on the required skills, knowledge, abilities, and tasks listed in the job description. For example, if a job description states that a position requires "multi-tasking" and is "fast-paced," this is usually a red blinking sign for you to run fast in the opposite direction! In addition, a job may require certain specific tasks that you find stressful, such as giving shots, working with blood, working with big dogs, or even just constant interaction with customers in person or via the phone. It is vital to be aware of your emotional stressors and search for jobs that will be a good emotional fit for you.

STORY

Rob was interning as a ranch hand when a baby cow was being birthed. Unfortunately, the calf got hurt and the ranch staff were not sure if it would survive. With reassurance from a job coach, Rob was able to work through that difficult moment, but he still perseverated on the experience and continued to process it with CIP staff in the upcoming days. In the end, he went to his career coordinator and said that he did not think being a ranch hand was the right career for him.

Another example is Marissa. Marissa was a student who had never interned or worked anywhere. She was anxious about the thought of *any* internship and often broke down crying, so finding the right emotional fit was extremely important. Marissa loved animals, and together we decided that an internship at a local animal shelter might be a good emotional fit. On her first day, something happened before her internship that upset her and elevated her anxiety. It almost looked like the internship would never happen—but with the help of her coach Marissa processed her emotions and was reassured that there would be a job coach and another student with her to show her the ropes and she was able to work through it.

She interned at the shelter for over a year and progressed to working without the need for a job coach. In fact, she became a strong mentor to the other students she worked with who turned to her for direction. Marissa learned that a career working with animals could be a good emotional fit for her—she just might need extra support and training when starting out a new job, regardless of the career focus.

—*Jennifer Kolarik, Career Coordinator, CIP Brevard*

EXERCISE

EMOTIONAL FIT CHECKLIST

List your emotional assets in the left column and your emotional challenges in the right column. Then prioritize them from 1 to 10, with 1 being the most important.

Emotional assets	Emotional challenges

PART II

Eight Skills Employers Look For

COMMUNICATION

TECHNOLOGY

TEAMWORK

8 SKILLS MOST IMPORTANT TO EMPLOYERS

PROBLEM SOLVING/ CRITICAL THINKING

WILLINGNESS TO LEARN

INITIATIVE AND LEADERSHIP

SELF- MANAGEMENT

PLANNING AND ORGANIZING

CHAPTER ONE

Communication

"Who is wise? He that learns from every one."

Benjamin Franklin[1]

Communication refers to the exchange of thoughts, messages, or information through speech, signals, writing, or behavior. There is more to it than just conveying a message. Who you are and how you are being with people is often more important than what you are saying. You need to check for understanding: to identify whether your message is being understood by someone exactly the way you intended it. You must also listen to expand the full meaning of what has been said, and then make the other individual feel heard and understood.

Communication is a necessary tool, yet it is a skill that is learned, not inherited. At the same time, it is of the utmost importance. Communication is the glue that connects you with everything: your job, your living space, and your relationships. You cannot be independent without others, and you cannot work with others without good communication skills.

It is also important to determine the appropriate communication style for your workplace. We may wonder about how much information we should share about ourselves, or about our Learning Differences. The answers to these questions are all determined by context. For example, if you are attending a college class, you may need to disclose to your professor how your Learning Difference affects you in the classroom to get the accommodation you need.

STRENGTHS IN COMMUNICATION

Here are some important areas to concentrate on when you are developing your communication skills.

HONESTY

When asked a question, will you reply with honesty? It is important to be honest while at the same time maintaining a diplomatic communication style. There is value in truth, but take care that your comments are not interpreted as rude by fellow colleagues. Also, understand the setting, and be careful not to share too much personal information.

CONFIDENCE

Confidence is a strong trait in the workplace and should be used to communicate your new ideas. Speak up on projects and share your ideas. Your opinion might have value if it's shared correctly. If you are receiving positive evaluations and are looking to move into a new position in the workplace, communicate to your manager that you are ready for more responsibility. You may be surprised by a promotion. Be confident when dealing with customers as well. Be polite and yet assertive when dealing with aggressive clients.

STORY

Jessie worked as a receptionist at an interior design firm that dealt with high-end homeowners. She often fielded calls from overly aggressive clients who wanted immediate action on their concerns. Jessie was somewhat passive and had to learn to be friendly but assertive at the same time. Her boss practiced critical situations with her to help her be polite but assertive.

FEEDBACK AND CONSTRUCTIVE CRITICISM

Use these powerful tools in the workplace to increase work efficiency and overall productivity. Most employers will provide you with quick back-and-forth comments. If you are not comfortable with this style, then instead of becoming disengaged, communicate to your manager a tailored approach that fits your style. For example, you might say, "I need clear feedback on what I am doing wrong and direct instruction on how the process should have been performed."

STORY

Oli was hired as an assistant to the butcher at a local meat market. He was very knowledgeable regarding the butchering process and the various cuts of meat, but he had a hard time accepting feedback from the boss, who was very structured in implementing safety procedures regarding the use of knives and hygiene in the market. After cutting himself a couple of times, however, Oli decided to accept the boss's feedback and constructive criticism.

HUMOR

There is a time and place for humor; know your environment. It is true that individual workplaces may be filled with sarcasm or jokes, but do not assume that everyone will respond favorably to your humor. A better approach is conveying positivity and a sense of optimism. These are the same characteristics embraced by fellow colleagues.

AUDIENCE

Know your audience and understand the platform you are communicating within. Are you replying to associates, managers, stakeholders, or potential clients? Make certain your language does not discriminate, especially if you are seeking to build a friendly atmosphere in the workplace.

PROACTIVITY

No matter the career path you choose, at some point you will encounter an unhappy moment in the workplace with a policy, procedure, or process regarding the way a situation has been handled. Do not respond to your employer out of frustration, let the problem persist, or assume that you should be speaking with top-level management. Instead, identify the problem right away, think clearly about how to solve it, and open a positive, engaging dialogue with the appropriate person in the company's established chain of command. Even though you live in a fast-paced world, rewards and gratification from your job may not come quickly. Instead, you should be proactive in helping to solve problems yourself.

STORY

Ryan worked as a maintenance assistant at a city housing project. He had several bosses who gave him conflicting agendas for the work he was to accomplish. Ryan started to get frustrated and upset. He decided to make a master list of all the work that needed to be accomplished and to be proactive in bringing his bosses in agreement with it.

PATIENCE

Show your employer that you have patience in your communication. As a product of immediate digital information 24/7, we sometimes forget traditional business timelines. Later in this chapter you will read a story of a young adult named Shayla who did not show patience when responding to their employer and requested an immediate response over the weekend.

STORY

Kelly was an employee of a local cheesemonger. Her boss, the owner, was very attentive to detail and tended to micromanage his employees. Kelly showed a lot of patience with him when he became anxious about an order or demanding about a task he wanted completed. She went about her work calmly and quietly and let him rant. He came to trust her and rely on her to be a calm force in the shop.

MULTI-TASKING

In the workplace, you may be asked to juggle many projects at once, or keep both short-term and long-term projects in mind. Keep a calendar and timeline so that you stay on track, and be sure to complete each task fully and to your utmost ability. But also beware: media devices have taught us the skills to juggle multiple conversations at the same time, and even though you have a capacity to answer the phone, reply to an email, and text all at the same time, your expert multi-tasking skills may not be appreciated in the workplace. It is important to understand that your employer could interpret this ability as not paying attention or lack of focus on a job task. Remember to stay on task.

TECHNOLOGY

Communication has changed drastically with millennials in the workforce. The traditional face-to-face office meeting and telephone conversation are being replaced by social media, email, texting, blogs, online chats, and video-conferences. New questions arise, such as whether it is appropriate to answer an advertisement for a job with a text. The answer is determined by context. For example, if an employer gives their cell phone number and asks you to send a text message, then you should follow suit. Outside of work, you must be aware that whatever you place on your Facebook page or on other social media sites can affect your success in gaining employment. You should strongly consider setting privacy restrictions on all social media sites you have a profile on, and ensure your information is not shared publicly.

It's also important to know the proper conventions for technological communication such as email. Start off by addressing the person to whom you are writing with their appropriate title (such as Ms., Mr., or Dr.), and sign off with your name. Be clear, specific, and polite in your message. Obey the rules of spelling, grammar, and punctuation, and proofread the message for typos before you send it.

STORY

In the following exchange, Nick sends a clear, honest, and proofread email to his employer, who takes notice of his excellent communication skills and decides to fulfill Nick's request.

Nick's letter

Mr. Johnson,

I just wanted to inform you of an issue I am having. I have trouble getting to my shift on Tuesday, on time and clean. My fitness class at the college ends at 12:45 and I need time to shower and get over to work.

I was hoping that you could give me a start time of 1:30 instead of 1pm. I would prefer to come to work clean and neat with my dress clothes on. This would give me time to shower and change and be on time to work. Any help you could provide regarding this would be most appreciated. If you require any additional information or input from me regarding this, let me know.

Sincerely,

Nick

Mr. Johnson's response

Dear Nick,

At first look at the schedules, I would typically respond "no" to your request because a change would affect other staff schedules (the staff schedules are tight this time of year). But because your request was so polite, rational, and had perfect tone, I have changed schedules to accommodate you. You can come in on Tuesdays at 1:30pm.

Mr. Johnson

—Michele Ramsay, Program Director, CIP Brevard

COMMUNICATION STYLE

Face-to-face communication does still occur in the workplace, and it is the most important form of communication there is. Therefore, you must understand the rules of communicating either in person or through screen sharing. At the moment that you are in face-to-face conversation, put away all devices (do not scan your cell phone or tablet for a text or email). Share your communication style with others. I prefer clear, direct, and collaborative communication!

STORY

Peter has difficulty with auditory processing and describes himself as someone who "tells it like it is" and isn't afraid to question authority. He has had difficulties in past internships when his overt honesty and questioning of assignments was viewed as "oppositional behavior" by his supervisor.

Aiden has challenges with self-advocacy. He disclosed frequently that he felt anxious at his last internship, especially when asking questions or requesting time off for medical reasons. He puts significant pressure on himself and carefully measures his words and interactions with others to avoid the potential of disappointing another person. He frequently appeases others and neglects his own needs.

These two students have varied communication styles and learned about their assets and deficits. Then, working together, they learned from each other how to advocate for their own needs during times of conflict. They accomplished this through a series of verbal discussions and written assignments regarding conflict resolution. They then used role-playing to exercise their communication skills. They learned to be direct and respectful in their communication.

—*Kelly Jamison, Career Coordinator, CIP Berkeley*

COMMUNICATION CHECKLIST

Rate yourself from 1 to 10 on the following, with 1 being the highest mark.

I speak with honesty and do my best to always tell the truth ☐

I am straightforward and honest but not too blunt ☐

I speak up when I have a question or concern ☐

I know the proper chain of command—the appropriate person for voicing my questions or concerns ☐

I listen when people offer feedback ☐

I am open to constructive criticism ☐

I maintain an optimistic attitude ☐

I only use humor when I know it's appropriate ☐

I alter my tone and subject matter depending on who I'm speaking to ☐

I am patient with others ☐

I can multi-task without being distracted ☐

I know how to use technological communication such as email or text messaging appropriately in the workplace ☐

I listen closely and make eye contact when communicating face-to-face ☐

I let the people I work with know the kind of communication style I prefer ☐

HOW TO DEVELOP BETTER COMMUNICATION

How do we improve communication? The answer is simple: practice! Practice the following skills at home for both social and professional situations. You can also have a job coach observe or record your communication skills on the job, then review them at home and practice the ones you need to work on the most.

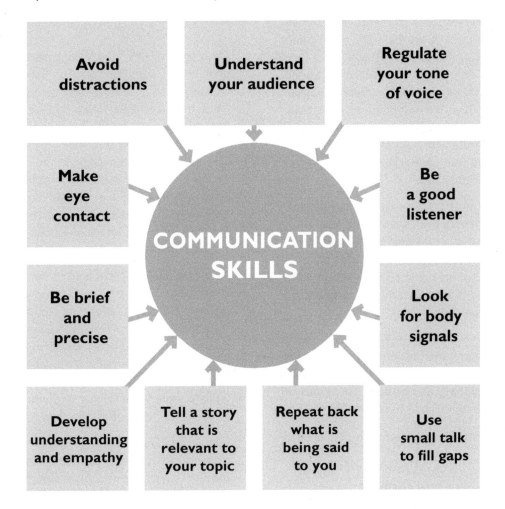

TIPS FOR PRACTICE

Avoid distractions

When speaking to someone, put away your cell phone, turn the TV or radio off, and hold your conversation away from others in a quiet locale.

Understand your audience

For example, you would speak differently to a child than you would to an adult. You would speak differently to your boss than you would your friend. Practice this at home.

Learn to regulate your tone of voice

Sometimes *how* you say something can be more effective than what you say. The old saying "You can attract more with honey than you do with vinegar" is a good mantra to keep in mind.

STORY

Peggy struggled to understand how her tone of voice drastically impacted how others received her feedback or instructions. When at her internship in a children's library, she did a great job providing a friendly customer service to library patrons and children. But when interacting with her co-workers, she often came across as snappy or negative. Peggy wore her emotions on her sleeve and her frustrations would come out in her tone of voice. Other times when she felt overwhelmed or frustrated, she avoided interaction with co-workers, thinking that would be a good approach, when in fact it made her co-workers think that she was rude and not a team player.

Peggy was not aware of how her communication might be perceived, but because she had a job coach to observe and provide feedback, Peggy was able to practice regulating her tone of voice at work. For example, if she said, "I'll take care of that," was her tone pleasant and confident, or was it sharp and edgy?

The good news was that Peggy very much wanted to become the best employee and team member that she could be, so she was willing to receive the feedback and made great strides in how she communicated with her team.

—*Jennifer Kolarik, Career Coordinator, CIP Brevard*

Make eye contact

Making eye contact in the workplace is especially important because it gives the listener (supervisor, co-worker, etc.) the impression that you are engaged and interested in what they are saying. Sometimes it can be uncomfortable to hold a gaze for too long, and it can also make others uncomfortable as well. Therefore, you may want to take a break from making eye contact about every five seconds (just shift your eyes away as if you were thinking about something). Also, to make you feel more comfortable,

you may want to shift your gaze. Once you become more comfortable with eye contact, add in some facial and body language (smiling, nodding your head, or raising your eyebrows) to reinforce the impression that you are actively listening.

STORY

Dave was a very nice young man but he had problems communicating. Dave became interested in numerous job opportunities and went on many interviews, but he had a great deal of difficulty in the interview process. He was always baffled when he never received a call offering him the position he sought. Dave lacked proper communication skills and his job coach worked with him to prep him for his next interview. Dave followed the advice, and with the refinement of just a few skills, he was able to procure a position he was interested in.

At work Dave still had a great deal of difficulty articulating what he was involved in and his feelings. He didn't listen well to others. When his employer spoke, Dave would seldom if ever make eye contact, and he had to be asked to take out the ear buds that were connected to his phone. Dave was also very distracted while people were talking, and would pay more attention to the distraction than to customers.

Lucky for Dave, he had an employer who understood his value at work and contacted the job coach to continue to refine Dave's skills on the job. He was able to change his communication style and continue to work on his skills to remain employed.

Be a good listener

Regardless of whom you are talking to or the topic, take the time and make a concerted effort to pay attention to the words that are directed at you. Practice at home, with your friends, family, and even strangers that you may have a brief conversation with.

STORY

Simon said he learned this lesson the hard way when he was frustrated with a current situation with his roommate who had been lashing out at him by cursing and speaking very disrespectfully. He thought the problem stemmed from his roommate thinking that he always had to be right. He realized that he did not listen well.

"I used to be like that," Simon said. "When I failed college the first time, I blamed many different things but didn't take responsibility for myself. After failing at a second college, I began to realize that I didn't know everything, and I wanted to learn from my support system how to be successful."

The bottom line: Simon learned that not only did he need to take responsibility, but it was also vital that he listened to those around him in a respectful way. And he completely changed the way he treated people. Now he is a source of positivity and support for all of his fellow students and co-workers.

—Jennifer Kolarik, Career Coordinator, CIP Brevard

Be brief and precise

Don't beat around the bush. Get straight to the point and be brief, especially if time is of the essence. Again, practice. If you want something, come right out and ask—without being too blunt.

Tip: Say it straight or it comes out crooked!

Look for body signals

How is your communicator's body language? For that matter, how is yours? Often a conversation can be ended before it even starts. If your arms are crossed and your shoulders are hunched, it gives the immediate impression that you are defensive or bored. If you're smiling, standing up straight, and looking at the person you're talking to, it gives the impression that you are interested and paying attention. Look for these signs in everyday situations, and practice good posture and positive body language.

STORY

Shayla, newly employed as a graphic design assistant, notices her schedule at work will conflict with her college class schedule. Since her boss asked employees to email him with any requests for schedule changes, Shayla sends him the following email: "This schedule is not going to work for me. I leave my class at 11:30. I need to have time to go back to my apartment and eat. I am flexible, but I cannot get around this."

The boss responds over the weekend during his off hours: "Give me an opportunity on Monday to try and move your schedule around to accommodate a later start time." Shayla, quite fixated on solving the problem immediately, responds: "You need to do more than fix it for that day; I don't want any start times before 1:00. I need time to have lunch and breathe. And please have my evening shift removed. I did not have that since the beginning of this year and feel that it must be a mistake. I have told my parents, and they agree with me. Please fix this."

The boss responds over the weekend: "Meet me in the office on Monday!" Shayla, while she thought she was being direct and not beating around the bush, was too blunt in her response to the supervisor. What do you think the supervisor said to her on Monday when they met in the office?

—Michele Ramsay, Program Director, CIP Brevard

Develop understanding and empathy

Understanding even the unspoken parts of your communication with others helps you respond more efficiently. Know the individual you are talking to. They may be having a bad day, or they might be tired of the problems consuming them. So tone it down if need be and practice finding out little details about people you know, so you have a better understanding of how to approach them.

Tell a story that is relevant to your topic

Telling a story is a great lead into your conversation, as long as it is relevant to your topic. Take your time before you speak and think of little anecdotes that are relevant to your conversation. Practice with friends and family. For example, start the conversation with: "The craziest situation popped up today…"

Repeat back what is being said to you

Repeating what a person says can be a critical communication tool. It shows the person speaking to you, that you heard them and understand what they are saying. Don't get me wrong: I'm not saying to repeat every word. Instead, when the person you are communicating with takes a moment to pause, say, "So what you mean is…" This will let the person you are communicating with know that you were listening and just want to clarify things with them. This also leaves no room for error when something is being said. Practice with friends and family. Say, "So Dad, what you mean is, I can take the car and stay out all night?" Get the idea? There is no room for a mistake when you repeat.

Use small talk to fill gaps

Practice small talk with everyone. A simple "How are you?" or "How is the family?" can go a long way towards getting a person into the right frame of mind when you speak with them. It will make them realize you are a caring person and someone they can talk to.

Communication skills can be practiced every day in settings that range from the social to professional. New skills take time to refine, but each time you use your communication skills, you open yourself to opportunities and future partnerships.

EXERCISE

IMPROVING COMMUNICATION

There are many ways to improve communication skills. Below are some simple communication exercises that can be practiced at any time; the point of these exercises is to start a connection dialogue. Select the ones that work best for you and put them to use, and above all, practice, practice, practice.

1. GIVE AND TAKE

Do this with a friend or family member.

- One person says a declarative sentence to you. Example: "I had the greatest time last night."

- The next person builds on that statement: "Really? What made last night so special?"

- Continue until each person has made five comments.

2. BREAKING THE ICE

You can do this with a classmate or friend. Use these starter questions to have a reciprocal conversation.

- In school: "Did you understand everything the professor spoke about?" "That was an excellent lecture—what did you take from it?"

- At work: "What are you going to do this weekend?" "How was your weekend?"

- At home: "How was your day?" "What are you going to do today?"

3. PRACTICE FOR AN INTERVIEW

Find a family member who can act as a potential employer. Have them ask these types of questions:

- "Can you tell us a time when you showed leadership?"

- "What is one of your proudest achievements?"

- "How would you manage a crisis?"

Improving Communication continues

4. BODY LANGUAGE

Observe others when you are out in society. What kind of body language do you see exhibited? When should you stand straight? How should you sit in a chair? How should you project your voice? Decide the proper posture for every situation from interviews to casual or professional work situations.

Play the Matching Game. Match the most appropriate item in the left column by drawing a line to its matching item in the right column.

Shake hands and introduce yourself	Meeting a bishop
Bow and kiss his ring	Meeting an employer
Give a hug	Meeting the Queen
Curtsy or bow	Meeting your aunt

5. VOCABULARY

Develop a list. Learn a new word that pertains to your job every day. Use it in context and use it at least once when you are speaking to others. Decide how it should be employed. Write down your new employment words on index cards and carry them in your pocket so you can refer to them throughout the day.

EFFECTIVE WORKPLACE COMMUNICATION

The following methods are the best ones to use when communicating with others in any workplace setting. Your supervisor, co-workers, and work team members will understand what you have to say, they will be clear about your intent, and they will appreciate your directness and clarity.

- One-on-one
- Emails
- Presentations
- Displaying confidence and seriousness
- Using simple words
- Listening to your co-workers and team members
- Using appropriate body language
- Using an appropriate tone of voice
- Avoiding unnecessary repetition
- Creating a receptive atmosphere
- Being humorous
- Being articulate
- Avoiding mumbling
- Encouraging feedback
- Gesticulating
- Being appreciative

CHAPTER TWO

Teamwork

"If I have seen further, it is by standing on the shoulders of giants."

Isaac Newton[2]

It is important to view your colleagues on the job as "teammates" working together to accomplish the goals of the business at hand. Imagine the construction of a building: architects who envision the plans coordinate with engineers to make sure the building is structurally sound; contractors cost-out materials and create timetables for construction; then various carpenters, masons, and roofers complete the structure. Each member of the team accomplishes their own role and coordinates their work with the other members, communicating and working together for a successful project. If you have information or knowledge that will bring the common effort forward, do not hoard it for personal gain at a later date. Share your ideas and thoughts and collaborate with colleagues to accomplish the business's mission and goals. This will also help you personally move ahead in the workplace and provide additional opportunities to show your skills and talents.

Sometimes it may seem easier just to do everything yourself. Individuals on the spectrum often have huge areas of special interest and technical knowledge, but they may lack the real-life, on-the-job experience to carry out their ideas. Instead, you need support, feedback, and flexibility to accomplish your mission. As individuals, we can be creative and correct about many things, or have a case of "terminal uniqueness," thinking the rules don't apply to us—yet, although "lone rangers" can sometimes come up with remarkable ideas, they usually can't accomplish what a group of brains can by working together. Individuals are fallible. Common sense often eludes us, and we make mistakes; however, when we listen to our teammates and check our work with them, it prevents us from making those mistakes that we'll later have to undo.

> Tip: When we work in harmony and in relationship with others, it may take longer to accomplish a goal, but the outcome is usually much better, and everyone is on board to carry it out.

HOW TO DEVELOP BETTER TEAMWORK

We get better at teamwork the same way we get better at communication: practice! Practice the following skills at home, at school, with friends, in study groups, and in your current work position.

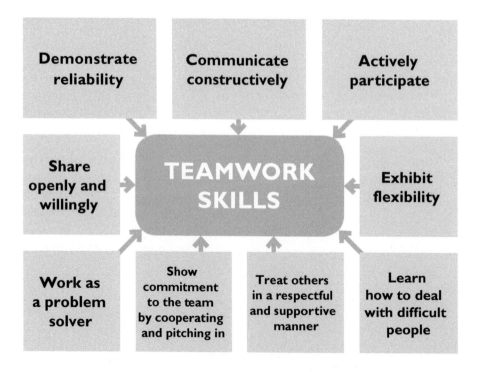

TIPS FOR PRACTICE

Demonstrate reliability

Consistency and perseverance often come easily to those on the spectrum or with Learning Differences. It is important to us to show up and be on time and to do what we say we will do. Our employers want to count on us to get done what they want, when they want, and with a consistent quality. This is a skill area that can make up for deficits in other areas. It is worth a lot to an employer to know that they can rely on us to be there and do a thorough job every time.

> *Tip: Show reliability and do what you say you will do.*

STORY

Emmy worked in a café that served breakfast and lunch. Her boss worked hard, coming in early to set up even with several small children at home. Emmy was an early riser and offered to learn the morning set-up routine so her boss could come in later a couple days of the week. After a few months, Emmy received a raise and became a shift manager. Her boss came to rely on her.

But who wants to get moving at 7am to shower, dress appropriately, eat breakfast, and drive to work? It feels much better to just sleep until whenever you feel like waking up! To hold down a job, you must wake up early and show up at the same time reliably each day. If you don't, it won't matter that you were successful in college and obtained a degree.

STORY

Dale struggled to make it to all of his appointments, especially his first morning appointments (at 8am or 9am). To help himself get on track, Dale took the following steps:

1. He decided how much sleep his body needs (8 hours or more typically) and what time he will need to wake up in the morning to be on time (thinking about all the tasks he must perform), then calculated, what time he needs to go to bed to get the right amount of sleep.

2. He set alarms (on his phone or an alarm clock).

3. He created an evening routine of setting out clean, wrinkle-free clothes, packing his lunch, and laying out his keys, wallet, and everything else he needs, so that the transition in the morning was much smoother.

4. He asked staff to call him in the morning on days that he slipped up.

One significant motivator for Dale was the performance evaluation completed by his work supervisor. Dale truly wanted to succeed and receive a good score. So when he was rated "needs improvement" for his attendance and punctuality, he was very disappointed. However, his motivation and effort increased and eventually he received a rating of "average" and then "above average" as he demonstrated progress.

Every now and then, Dale slips up and oversleeps. Most of the time, he handles it responsibly by calling his work supervisor, and then taking the bus to his internship if he missed his ride. However, on several occasions Dale has made a monumental mistake: a "no call, no show." This is certainly a ground for dismissal from a job. And Dale has had to face the music when his internship supervisor called him to ask where he was.

Luckily for Dale, his internship site knows that he is working on certain personal challenges and they are willing to help him work through these difficult moments…but it will be important for him to overcome this last lesson in reliability before transitioning to a paid job!

Communicate constructively: Actively listening and asking questions

Communication can be one of the greatest challenges for young adults on the spectrum. We talked about how important it is to have good communication skills with our employer and fellow employees in our last chapter, but it's worth reminding ourselves that creating an open climate is very important to the workability of the group. So, whenever you're at work, be sure to make eye contact, use an appropriate tone of voice, and listen carefully, repeating back what your employer or co-worker has said to be sure you're both on the same page. If you don't understand something, have the courage to keep asking for clarification so that you understand.

> *Tip: All questions and all answers are intelligent, because they bring you closer to understanding what you don't know.*

STORY

Stan was told by his boss to put away the refrigerator and freezer order that would arrive at the store early that morning. The boss said he would return later in the afternoon. When the order arrived, Stan noticed that the boxes were cold and the label on the top box read "butter," so he put all the boxes in the refrigerator.

When his boss returned, he noticed that the whole order was in the refrigerator. The boxes on the bottom, however, were clearly marked "ice cream" and had totally thawed out. They were ruined. Stan could have avoided this mistake if he'd actively listened when his boss told him to put away the refrigerator *and freezer* order.

Actively participate

There is a balance between not participating at all and over-participating. While some young adults on the spectrum struggle with nearly any form of communication (especially verbal face-to-face), others struggle with communicating TMI (too much information). Ever heard the expression "he talked my ear off"? If you are a member of a work team, you need to know the balance. For example, if you are the "new kid on the block" then you should wait and listen for a while before you participate. If you speak up too soon or say too much, you can alienate the other team members. On the other hand, you cannot stay back and be quiet forever. You will quickly lose your value to the team if you do not speak up when you have something valuable to contribute.

This is a delicate balance and you must use all the social thinking skills you have to read the non-verbal cues of your team members. You must be able to infer when they are looking for information from you. You must be able to interpret their responses accurately to know if they want you to continue on or stop. You need to learn the "office politics." Who thinks they are in charge? Who is easily offended? Who has a big ego and always wants to save face? Which tone of voice should you use with which colleagues? When is someone being humorous and not being serious? All of these will impact your effectiveness and image on the team. One solution is to find allies on and off the team who can mentor you and steer you in the right direction.

> *Tip: Identify allies who can assist you on the job.*

STORY

For Shelly, participating actively came easy—in fact, too easy. In her position as an admissions assistant, she shared *everything*, and believed that others wanted to hear it. Unfortunately, nothing could have been further from the truth. During meetings, Shelly would frequently interject with her observations and recommendations. She would frequently speak over staff who were speaking with students, families, and professionals. Shelly came away from each experience energized and believing that she did a great job! Unfortunately, admissions staff walked away frustrated that they could not complete their sentences or finish their points. Her active participation was welcome; however, monopolizing everyone's time or boring them to tears with over-participation was not.

With the help of a job coach, Shelly learned how to edit the information she chose to share according to her audience (supervisor vs. co-worker vs. friend) and the amount of information to be shared (e.g., relaying a general account of a customer interaction instead of a detailed eyewitness description). She became more respectful of the other person's availability by asking questions like "Is this a good time?" and "How much time do you have?" If her boss only has five minutes before an important meeting and she needs to give him an update, she now decides which important facts have to be conveyed and quickly gives an overview, while skipping the detailed accounts of someone's hair color, what type of ice cream they were eating, and all the other small details.

—*Jennifer Kolarik, Career Coordinator, CIP Brevard*

Share openly and willingly

On most teams, being transparent and open about your thoughts will benefit the team and yourself. Being willing to help and work with others on the team is the best thing to do. If you think someone is going to take credit for your ideas then you should only share those ideas inside the team and not outside with a non-team member. Seek out other team members that you feel you can confer with safely and who will respect your ideas and give you credit when you express them outside of a meeting.

STORY

Sean was timid in a group setting and not a self-promoter, but he freely shared his ideas with his colleague, Frank. One staff meeting, Frank shared one of Sean's ideas and took credit for it as his own. Sean became angry as Frank got approval from the boss, but he became passive-aggressive and wouldn't say anything. Sean's employer picked up on this and sent him on a six-week night course, based on the book *How to Win Friends and Influence People* by Dale Carnegie. This helped Sean to learn confidence and to speak up and assert himself at meetings.

Exhibit flexibility

Flexibility is perhaps the most important skill in working with others. You can exhibit flexibility in a number of areas, such as scheduling, job requirements, helping your teammates, and adjusting to changes in personnel or procedure. It's especially important to be flexible and open to others' ideas about how to accomplish a task. Every project can be approached in many ways, and we must be able to hear and evaluate diverse opinions and ideas that might lead to a better solution than the one we were so sure of.

Being flexible does not mean giving up on your creative idea, but you must communicate it to others in a manner that allows them to see its value. If they decide that your idea is not the best, then you have to negotiate, compromise, or accept the new idea and let go of your approach for the time being. Your thinking may be too far beyond the understanding of the team, or you may not see the implications of what you are proposing. A healthy debate in most teams is fine, but when you insist that your solution is the only solution, then you better have the facts and rationale to prove that or be willing to let it go.

Tip: Remain open and flexible to others' ideas.

STORY

George's supervisor ran into a problem with an order that was going to arrive the next day, half an hour after she had to leave to pick up her son at school. George overheard her trying to figure out a solution with another employee, so he spoke up and offered to stay half an hour late to receive the order. George's boss was so grateful for his flexibility that she told him he could sleep in an extra hour in the morning and come in late.

Show commitment to the team by cooperating and pitching in

Dedicated team members get things done and do them without needing to be dragged into it. They anticipate what others need, and do what they can to make the process easier for everyone involved. Think about a time when you were approaching a door with your hands filled to the brim, and a co-worker offered to open the door for you. Or better yet, they even asked if you had more items in your car that you could use help carrying in. The skill of cooperating and pitching in requires not only social thinking (what might your co-worker need?) but also the skill of taking initiative, anticipating a need, and offering assistance before someone asks you for it.

Sometimes you have to work with people that you don't really care for or don't feel close to, but you must be able to put aside those feelings and work for the common good. Employers want employees who work well together to accomplish tasks in a timely manner. If someone is constantly bickering or disrupting the team, the whole process can be undermined. Develop a one-for-all and all-for-one attitude and you will win over colleagues and influence people.

You can form partnerships and alliances with others to support each other in attaining goals. These are agreements for mutual benefit and move both partners forward in their goals.

STORY

Cooperation was Garrison's greatest strength. Not only did he do what was asked of him at his zoo internship, but also he always asked what else his supervisors needed assistance with. Because of that, they turned to him not just for animal care tasks, but also for handyman or deep cleaning tasks. In turn, this provided him with greater opportunities to strengthen and broaden his set of job skills. They began to think of him as Mr. Fix-It. He made himself an invaluable member of that team by making it known that he was there to help!

—*Jennifer Kolarik, Career Coordinator, CIP Brevard*

Work as a problem solver

Anticipate problems that will get in the way of your team accomplishing its goal, and then be part of the solution! Small things matter a lot in making the team work freely and without disruption, such as arranging the meeting room, making sure the proper supplies are there, communicating schedule changes, and notifying others of important information.

Tip: Be proactive in anticipating solutions.

STORY

Tim worked at a recycling plant for two months. He noticed that on rainy days the outside recycling bins would become filled with water and had to be emptied out before they could be processed. He also noticed that there was a large overhang on the side of the building that was used to store plastic containers that had holes in the bottom of them.

Each morning the employees had a ten-minute "stand up" meeting with Mrs. Ackerman, the Chief Sanitation Engineer. One morning, Tim suggested that if they moved the recycling bins under the overhang and the plastic containers with holes in them were put out into the open, then they would not have to empty the water out of the recycling bins and would have a dry product to process. This suggestion was welcomed and implemented by the supervisor, making the team's work much more efficient. Tim received the Employee of the Month award for this suggestion.

Supervisors are continually looking for individuals who not only complete the required job tasks but do so without being told and look for additional ways to pitch in. You must first recognize that there is a need, and then be confident enough to take the initiative to meet that need. Volunteering to get some work done outside the group or taking on leadership roles to organize or complete a task will make you an invaluable team member. See the following chapter, "Problem Solving and Critical Thinking," for more advice!

Tip: Be part of the solution.

STORY

Ethan was always pointing out problems and how things did not work on the job. His supervisor got tired of hearing this constantly and finally instituted a new rule at work for all the employees. The supervisor said: "From now on, if anyone brings up a problem at staff meeting, then they must present at least two possible solutions for us to consider. I am paying you all for your intelligence and knowledge on the job. You all have the brains and degrees to come up with possible solutions." Problem solved!

Treat others in a respectful and supportive manner

Maintaining professional distance and respectful speech is important in a group. Some people may be able to joke around, but if that is not your strength, you are better off staying positive, making supportive statements to others, and keeping a respectful profile. We risk being offensive if we joke around with others, especially before we know them well or

understand the group dynamics. Don't listen to or repeat gossip; you never know who will quote you and to whom.

STORY

Kasey, a student from Vermont (and an ardent Phish Phan!), was well liked in her job working at a nutrition program for children on the Autism Spectrum. She always had a good word to say about other employees and the clients she worked with. She stayed clear of controversy and did not repeat gossip, and she earned the trust of all the other employees. When she spoke up at staff meetings people listened because she had earned their respect.

Using appropriate language can be exceptionally challenging for some of us who may use casual language with peers but then need to use more formal language in the workplace. You may find it difficult to shift from a casual to a more public mode.

STORY

Mark tended to curse a lot. He tried to keep it out of the workplace until one day when he accidentally slipped. His task was to call local businesses to promote the services offered at the local chamber of commerce. If he did not reach a live person, he was supposed to leave a voicemail. Leaving a message one day, he got flustered, said the wrong thing, and unfortunately blurted out a cuss word in exasperation. The person who heard the message was upset by the unprofessionalism and called Mark's CEO.

After sitting down with Mark, the company agreed to give him one more chance. They provided Mark with additional phone training and minimized his phone interactions for a while. This was definitely a learning opportunity that Mark would never forget—and he worked very hard to use respectful, work-appropriate language whenever at his internship or job.

—*Jennifer Kolarik, Career Coordinator, CIP Brevard*

Learn how to deal with difficult people

You may have to deal with supervisors and other employees who do not respect you. Some just may not like you—and you may not like them. It can be a difficult position to be in. You may need to seek advice from supervisors or management to figure out how to resolve difficult problems on the job.

STORY

Rich was training to be a security guard at a big box store. He was assigned two partners: Brad, a middle-aged heavy-set man who kept to himself, and Stan, an older man who had been hired six months before. Stan was a know-it-all and talked constantly, making bad jokes and gossiping about every other employee. After a couple days on duty, Rich was overwhelmed. He didn't know what to do. When they met with their supervisor, they did so as a group and Rich could not speak up to voice his concerns.

After another week passed, Rich asked to schedule a time with his supervisor to talk to him about the situation. He tactfully requested to be changed to another group if possible and politely explained his reasons. His supervisor understood his concern and shifted him onto another team of experienced and quieter guards.

STORY

Michael worked at a publishing company as a writer and had to work closely with the Chief Editor, Mrs. Fitton. She was a very precise and knowledgeable woman, and could be generous and kind, but if she perceived that anyone in the department made a mistake she would take it personally and verbally castigate and run them down in front of the rest of the team.

Michael was so fearful that he might make a mistake and get on her "bad side." He asked to talk confidentially to the Human Resources Director to share his concern and seek advice on how to deal with this situation. The HR Director gave him some advice and indicated that this was not new information to him. After a couple months, Mrs. Fitton suddenly resigned after getting some feedback from the president of the company that offended her.

EXERCISE

TEAMWORK

In their article "Skills for Graduates in the 21st Century,"* the Association of Graduate Recruiters revealed that the ability to work in a team was one of the top ten shortcomings for recent graduates. Yet employers rely heavily on teamwork from their employees for their business to succeed—and an effective team must be made up of employees with varying traits who will contribute to the company in different ways.

The traits below are important to being a good teammate. Check off your strengths. You can describe these traits to potential employers as an illustration of why you will make a good team member:

- [ ] I am a well-organized individual and good at keeping to deadlines.
- [ ] I help others find compromises between differing viewpoints.
- [ ] I introduce new ideas to groups in which I work.
- [ ] I act as the note-taker for the groups I am involved in.
- [ ] I suggest new ways of doing things.
- [ ] I'm positive in my approach and build on the ideas of others.
- [ ] I support and praise other team members.
- [ ] I use laughter to remove stresses in groups in which I work.
- [ ] I make sure all possibilities are explored.
- [ ] I try to keep relations between group members harmonious.
- [ ] I am an optimist who tends to look on the positive side.
- [ ] I act as the spokesperson, to deliver the findings of the group.
- [ ] I usually lead and coordinate the team effort.
- [ ] I think outside of the box and suggest ways of looking at problems.
- [ ] I encourage team members to work hard with positive energy.
- [ ] I summarize what was said and share my notes with the team.

---

*   Available at www.agr.org.uk/write/Documents/Reports/Skills__for_Graduates_in_the_21st_Century.pdf

RATE YOURSELF AS A TEAM PLAYER

	Always	Sometimes	Never
Gossip at work?			
Look for solutions on the job?			
Offer to help others?			
Talk behind someone's back?			
Make supporting remarks?			
Offer to assist?			
Make discouraging remarks?			
Speak up with my ideas?			
Attend meetings on time?			
Actively listen to others' ideas?			
Praise co-workers?			
Accept criticism?			
Fight for your ideas?			
Demonstrate flexibility?			

CHAPTER THREE

Problem Solving and Critical Thinking

"Change will not come if we wait for some other person, or if we wait for some other time. We are the ones we've been waiting for."

Barack Obama[3]

Learning how to solve problems rationally is integral to your success. Problems will arise at work, in your relationships, in public…everywhere other humans are! Learning how to deal with them will help you in every area of your life. Most problem-solving skills are developed through everyday life and experience. However, we cannot depend on learning every skill by trial and error, and although employers certainly will be patient, they can put up with only so many mistakes before they seek a change. Using rational problem-solving skills will assist you in getting the outcomes you want.

As you move through the steps below (Stop, Observe, Deliberate, and Act), remember to maintain a rational mindset. If a conflict or problem arises and you need to talk to your employer or a co-worker about it, keep your facial expression calm and neutral. Make eye contact with whomever you are speaking to, and speak clearly, deliberately, and without emotion. Don't shout or cry. Let the person know the facts about the problem *only*, not your opinion. Once both parties have spoken, you can negotiate in order to come up with a solution to the problem that will satisfy everyone. Be ready to compromise: you may not get everything you want, but you should feel somewhat content with the solution.

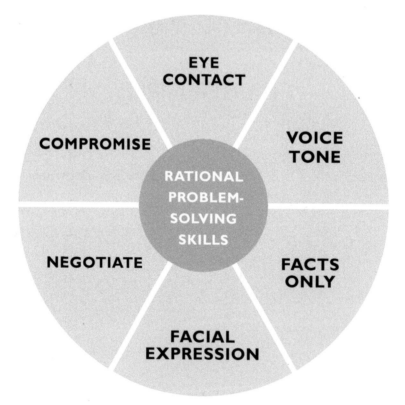

HOW TO STOP, OBSERVE, DELIBERATE, AND ACT

Think of your brain as a living bio-computer, making calculations and learning as it goes. All your colleagues have unique bio-computers with unique abilities and power. Sometimes scientists loop together a series of computers to gain the power and ability to work on complex data. You can use the information and problem-solving skills of other bio-computers to make solid decisions that you would not be capable of making on your own by utilizing those around you to help you solve problems.

The acronym SODA can be used to assist you with your critical-thinking and decision-making skills on the job. If you are stuck and don't know how to handle a problem, then, as we say, "take a SODA" to find a good solution.

STOP

Before you can work on solving a problem you need to stop what you are doing and calm down, so your ears and mind are open to understanding what is going on. Stop yourself from thinking about anything else and concentrate on trying to listen and think clearly. This can be a challenging and often painful process, but try to see the situation without fear and anxiety. The obstacles we encounter and changes we have to make are just part of life. Being calm and reading the situation will open the door to possible solutions. Remain open to the process of growth.

Tip: Look objectively, not emotionally, at what is really happening.

STORY

Manny has developed a set way of getting through his day. He is comfortable when his schedule is set, but like most of us it can be very challenging for him to work through obstacles. Manny interns at a local food pantry, and every day he knows what his supervisor expects of him. During his training Manny was shown how to cut bread with a long, serrated, green-handled knife. He did great with this. He was careful with the blade and divided the bread up into equal pieces. His supervisor was very impressed.

Each day at work, Manny starts off by cutting donated bread, but one day the long green-handled knife was not to be found. Manny faced a challenge. He wanted to please his boss and was afraid of doing the job incorrectly, but instead of seeking help, he just waited, staring at the uncut loaves of bread, standing next to an entire drawer filled with knives. When his supervisor arrived, it had already been 20 minutes and Manny had not done any work. This reflected poorly on his performance review, but it was a teachable moment and his job coach worked with him to resolve the problem.

—*Charles Culp, Career Coordinator, CIP Bloomington*

OBSERVE

Try to observe what is going on around you, who is present, what happened, and how you and others reacted to the situation.

- Gather information systematically: Who? What? When? Where?

- Collate and organize the data either in your head or on a piece of paper (like trying to recreate a crime scene!).

- Condense and collate information.

- Look beyond the obvious; what are the factors affecting this situation?

- Use the information gathered effectively by clarifying what exactly happened.

- Define the characteristics of the problem.

- Evaluate information and situations.

- Break the problem down into smaller, more manageable parts.

- Formulate questions.

- Sometimes what looks like a problem dissolves under scrutiny and we can see in the light of observation that it is not a problem at all.

> *Tip: As the detective on the old sitcom "Dragnet" used to say: "Just the facts ma'am."*

STORY

In Manny's case, he needed to stop and then observe what was going on around him (the drawer of knives, other staff, etc.). What time did his supervisor arrive? Was it in a couple minutes? Were there any other circumstances or situations that could affect this situation?

DELIBERATE

You've already thought critically about the problem by breaking it apart and analyzing it. Now, you need to deliberate in order to define the desired objective and come up with the best solution.

Define your objective

If you could have it your way, what would be the best outcome? What is your main objective? What are you trying to accomplish?

Decide on the best solution

- Consider various ways of approaching and resolving the problem.

- Brainstorm and list all the possible solutions you can think of (either in your head, or, if you have time, on paper).

- Critically examine your possible solutions.

- Run your solutions past trusted mentors (use the Donkey Rule below).

- Evaluate and select which alternatives fit best in solving the problem.

- Look at the disadvantages/barriers/obstacles to the solutions.

- Look at the advantages/effectiveness of the solutions.

- Look at the possible consequences/limits of each solution.

- Use the Donkey Rule again if necessary and poll your mentors to see what the consensus is.

THE DONKEY RULE

If five people call it a donkey, it is not a horse.

If five people you trust give you similar advice in a situation, you should probably go with their advice.

CHOOSING MENTORS

The key element is picking five people (mentors, advisors, teachers, family members, or mature adults) to ask an important question to before you make a decision, especially in critical situations.

FIVE MENTORS I CAN RELY ON FOR GOOD ADVICE:

1. _____

2. _____

3. _____

4. _____

5. _____

STORY

After he observed the situation as best he could, Manny could have deliberated and thought about possible solutions. Could he perform another task and come back to the bread after the supervisor arrived? Maybe there was a similar knife with a different-colored handle? Maybe there was another staff member or employee to ask where the knife was? Maybe he could ask another employee what he thought he should do, or ask more than one and come up with a solution?

ACT

Put the solution into action! Letting problems mount up is a recipe for disaster. It's like not washing your dishes for a month! You become overwhelmed and unable to face them or know where to start. It is important for your emotional health to solve problems as they occur on a daily basis and get used to meeting these challenges head-on.

Employers want to see initiative, but your plan needs to be well thought-out or you could make it worse. Implementing an action that you thought through with other employees is usually the best plan. Action has two parts: first, implement the solution; then, monitor the outcome.

STORY

In a better scenario, after deliberating or using the Donkey Rule, Manny would take action. If a couple other employees said "Just use the best knife you can find until we find the green-handled one," then he would have been completing his job when the supervisor arrived and then he could have explained the situation to her. Or maybe they would have suggested other actions, like texting her or doing another important task. In any case, he would have been in action: some work could have been accomplished, and the supervisor would usually applaud his initiative.

IMPLEMENT THE SOLUTION

- Decide if further information needs to be gathered before taking action.

- Make a step-by-step plan.

- Decide what resources you need (tools, time, money, materials, etc.).

- Gather your resources.

- Take the first step, then the next, then the next…

MONITOR THE OUTCOME

It is important to assess the outcome of your solution. You want to know if your solution was effective and whether you need to do anything more or change what you are doing the next time.

- Ask yourself: Did the chosen solution solve the problem?

- Ask yourself: Was the problem solved completely or are there remnants to be cleaned up?

- Implement a second solution if necessary.

- Review the problem and problem-solving process to help to avoid similar situations in the future. (Why keep repeating the same unsuccessful solutions over and over again? Remember the definition of insanity is doing the same thing over and over again and expecting different results.)

Tip: Follow through to completion.

STORY

Manny reviewed the outcome of his inaction and saw the consequences. The next time he faces this type of dilemma, he will use SODA to come up with and implement a solution. His performance review will then say: "Shows initiative in solving problems."

EXERCISE

SOLVING A PROBLEM

Name a situation in which you might get stuck on your job, internship, or community service site. Then use SODA to determine some solutions to implement.

Problem situation:

_____

_____

S: _____

O: _____

D: _____

A: _____

EXERCISE

PROBLEM RESOLUTION WORKSHEET

Identify five problems that you have faced at your internship or job site. Then describe the solution you implemented for each. Share your strategies and tips with your career support group or job coach.

Problem faced at internship/job	Solution used

CHAPTER FOUR

Initiative and Leadership

"It's not the critic who counts."

Theodore Roosevelt[4]

HOW TO DEVELOP INITIATIVE

When internship and job supervisors complete feedback forms regarding work performance, the number one area that needs improvement is the need to take initiative. Individuals on the spectrum often find that their comfort zone is in following directions. Once you have completed all work tasks, you may find it challenging to take initiative if you are unable to ask your supervisor what to do next, either because the supervisor is unavailable or because the supervisor wants you to determine the next step on your own.

Initiative is defined as displaying behavior that shows others you have a self-starting nature, can use a proactive approach when working with others, and will be persistent as you work to overcome day-to-day difficulties. Someone who shows initiative *acts* instead of *reacts* while working. Organizations want individuals who can take action without waiting for someone to tell them what to do.

STORY

Lillian was a very creative student and worked at a coffee shop for several months. She would arrive early to set up the coffee station with cream, sugar, agave syrup, stirrers, and other items. She noticed that, when customers ordered at the cash register, they had to back track to the table where these items were set. She took some initiative and moved the table past the cash register to an empty wall. She put a new tablecloth on top of the table and a chalkboard on which she wrote the clever message "Sweeten Your Day" in colored chalk.

When her boss arrived, Lillian took her to the table and said: "I thought this would be helpful, but if you want me to move it back I will." The boss was delighted with her initiative. She adjusted the table about a foot to the left and said: "This looks great. Thank you."

TIPS FOR PRACTICE

Build self-confidence

Developing the skills discussed in this part of the workbook (such as communication, teamwork, problem solving, and critical thinking) will go a long way towards building your self-confidence. With these skills, and the career portfolio and other documents you develop at the end of this book, you can take a look at all you have accomplished and all you are capable of. Remember that you are a valuable member of your class or work team.

Learn about workplace procedure

Take your time and learn as much as possible about how things work in your place of employment. As discussed in Lillian's story above, the more you know about how your workplace operates and the chain of command, the better you are able to see what tasks need to be completed, notice when something is going wrong and know how to fix it, spot someone who needs help and help them, and know who to ask about what to do next.

Spot opportunities for improvement

If you see a problem in the workplace or if you find yourself without work to do, take a SODA. Ask yourself or your job coach: How can this problem be solved? How can I be part of the solution? If you can't seem to complete a task, no matter how hard you try, ask yourself or your job coach: What skills do I need to work on in order to improve my workplace capabilities?

Sense-check your ideas

Be sure your solution is the right one before moving forward. Remember to SODA.

Develop rational persistence

If you are doing the same thing over and over again and not getting any results, that is *irrational* persistence. Change your methods in order to get results—and don't stop trying. Success is doing each small action well, and doing the right thing over and over again.

STORY

Ben was working on typing tests that recorded his typing speed and number of errors. He took the typing test six times and still had a pretty high error count. When his job coach mentioned to him that he was fast but needed to work on decreasing his errors, he revealed that he did not know that he could make corrections during the test, because his job coach did not explicitly *tell* him he could correct errors. If she didn't tell him, it didn't happen. Similar scenarios play out time and time again in the workplace.

Ben was doing the same thing over and over again and expecting different results. Instead of waiting for someone else to change his behavior, he should have taken the initiative to change it himself. If there is a problem in the workplace, or you are not achieving your goals, take the initiative to SODA (Stop, Observe, Deliberate, and Act). After doing poorly on one or two tests, Ben should have stopped and gathered himself; observed that his problem was too many typing errors; deliberated on possible solutions to correct the errors (like whether he could fix them as he took the test); and acted by correcting his typing errors as they happened.

—*Jennifer Kolarik, Career Coordinator, CIP Brevard*

Find balance

Take the right amount of initiative while still being a team player. Sometimes we act when we shouldn't, without thinking things through. If you are unsure if you should take initiative in some area, check it out with others—a co-worker, a mentor, a job coach, or a supervisor—before proceeding.

STORY

When our student Frank obtained a position as a clerical assistant, he was very anxious to please his new boss. One day, when there was a lag in work, he used his own initiative to seal the envelopes for a mailing that was being completed in the office. He assumed that he was being proactive and forward thinking; however, he did this without asking his supervisor, so he did not know that the mailing was incomplete, needing one more paper before being sealed. By rushing forward and sealing the envelopes, he inadvertently cost the business many hours of additional work. He thought he was being a "self-starter," but in reality he did not yet know enough about the office protocol to accomplish this.

Frank decided to learn more about the chain of command and how his office worked (see the section 'Learn about workplace procedure' above). He learned that, if he had free time, asking for additional work was the route he needed to take. Frank learned that it was fine to be a self-starter but only if he paid attention to the tasks at hand, communicated with others, and learned to do his job correctly. His career coordinator provided him with a list of five tasks he could work on if he ran out of work. Those tasks were agreed upon and endorsed by his employer.

HOW TO DEVELOP LEADERSHIP SKILLS

Leadership is the act of guiding a group of people. However, being a leader does not mean that you have to be in a leadership or supervisory role in the workplace. Below we describe how you can be a leader whatever your position.

Integrity · Openness · Inspiration · Curiosity · **QUALITIES OF A LEADER** · Courage · Ambition · Creativity · Honesty · Networking

THE QUALITIES OF A LEADER

- *Integrity:* Honor the principles and morals that you strongly stand for in your actions and words.

- *Openness:* Listen carefully to the words of others.

- *Inspiration:* Influence others by setting a good example, leading with your actions, not with your words.

- *Curiosity:* Ask questions and seek out new knowledge.

- *Courage:* Be brave enough to speak up and take initiative.

- *Ambition:* Have the desire to improve and succeed.

- *Creativity:* Think "outside of the box" to solve problems.

- *Honesty:* Tell the truth.

- *Networking:* Make connections with others.

> *Tip: Say what you mean, and mean what you say.*

STORY

Although Sam did not see himself as a leader, his depth of work experience and skills put him in a leadership role very quickly at his internship at the university's science lab. In fact, after interning for just one term, he was offered a paid position. When staff and volunteers needed help, they often came to him for instruction, asking, "Is this the right way to do this? How should I do this?" Sam began to make lists to help them prioritize their work tasks. His supervisor asked him to train all new volunteers and staff because she trusts that he will do a good job. Whenever she goes on vacation, she lists him as the point of contact for staff who have questions—and stipulates that volunteers can only work when Sam is working.

Even though he did not have a formal title or position, Sam was a "backseat" leader. His title was the same as the other staff whom he was directing. On one performance evaluation, his supervisor said that she would like for him to step up even more as a leader...so he took it to heart. It was as if he had been given the "green light." So instead of waiting for others to come to him, Sam took note when staff or volunteers were sitting around not knowing what to do and he began to direct them without being told to do so. He is currently planning to transition to another paid position at a local hospital and has begun thinking about how he can help prepare the other staff and volunteers for his departure. He has been writing up many Standard Operating Procedures (SOPs)—sets of step-by-step instructions to help other co-workers carry out procedures.

Sam has also been taking the initiative to teach a "hidden curriculum" to his co-workers about what their supervisor's preferences (or pet peeves) might be. For example, he has one co-worker who runs to her for every little thing, which can be time-consuming and overwhelming for a supervisor. He recommended that the co-worker think about the chain of command and turn to him or another co-worker first, rather than making his supervisor his "first stop." He suggested that his co-worker could write down all of his questions and take them to their supervisor just once a day rather than every few minutes.

—*Jennifer Kolarik, Career Coordinator, CIP Brevard*

EXERCISE

INITIATIVE AND LEADERSHIP

Form a small group of people. For each of the following situations come up with a solution you would implement:

Your office has several employees out with the flu and others are complaining of symptoms. What would you do?

_____

_____

An employee was mentioned in the local newspaper as having been named volunteer of the year for the local Red Cross. What would you do?

_____

_____

The employee bathroom is being used by customers who leave it dirty and in a mess. What would you do?

_____

_____

Your restaurant is having less foot traffic since a new restaurant opened down the street. What would you do?

_____

_____

CHAPTER FIVE

Planning and Organizing

"The organized rule the world."

Michael McManmon[5]

HOW TO PLAN AND ORGANIZE

Planning and organizing are the backbone of executive functioning, or cognitive (brain-based) activities such as logic, strategy, problem solving, information processing, and behavior control. I know from my own challenges of being on the spectrum how difficult it can be to plan my time, meet deadlines, and organize my work and myself.

When you enter the working world, the key is to show your employer that you can prioritize, work efficiently and productively, and manage your time well. In this chapter, we will help you develop the planning and organizing skills you will need to master these executive functioning abilities.

Tip: Excellence is arising each day and doing the most difficult tasks first, then rewarding yourself later in the day with doing the things you love. It is a habit of facing up and not being afraid to handle problems.

STORY

Mike was diagnosed with ADD and worked in an office as a case manager for students on the spectrum. He had good social skills and worked well with his students, but he had a hard time staying seated in his office, prioritizing tasks, and completing his paperwork and reports.

Mike decided to try a few things to help with his executive functioning. When he needed a break from the office, he would sometimes walk around the block with the students he needed to talk to. In order to help him focus, he completed 15 sessions of biofeedback therapy with a local psychologist. He used an organizer and calendar to prioritize his work each day, and his desk slowly became organized. He broke down his reports and long-term projects and did some work on them every day, and he used the last half hour of every workday to get out of his work area and organize for the next day. Finally, on Fridays, he took the last hour to do some thorough cleaning and organizing so that he could enjoy his weekend and come into work the next week and start fresh!

TIPS FOR PRACTICE

Plan your day and week

When you first start a job or internship, your supervisor will discuss your duties with you: which tasks you must complete, how long each task takes, and when each task must be completed. Meeting these requirements will be your primary goal at work, so you will need to plan your workday so that tasks are accomplished. Set goals and create a timeline for accomplishing your goals. Each morning, decide which tasks are most important and what needs to be done to meet deadlines. A task that is supposed to take five months to complete becomes much more doable if the employee has a target and a timeline to adhere to. This might mean reporting on progress to the employer every two weeks until the goal is met.

Tip: Find out the priority for the day from your supervisor and work on that first.

STORY

The publisher of this book gave me a deadline for getting the manuscript to them. We did an outline of the book first (the prelims, chapters, conclusion, and end matter). We broke down each chapter into sub-headings. Within each area we decided to have a narrative regarding the topic, a tip or advice, a relevant story, and an exercise.

We then divided the workload, meeting every couple months for two full days of writing and editing. Throughout the process, we had a marketing assistant put the document in the publishing format, make graphics, etc. After we assembled a full document, we then had an editor go through it to put it all in the same voice, correct for spelling and grammar, and add some additional writing ideas for us. The last part of the process was to reread the draft several times, improving it and making it flow correctly, before submitting it to the publisher.

Tip: Take the time to plan out your work for the week.

EXERCISE

PREPARING FOR WORK CHECKLIST

Use this form to organize yourself each evening or morning.

	Mon	Tues	Wed	Thurs	Fri	Sat	Sun
Backpack organized?							
Cell phone charged?							
Keys?							
Laptop?							
Pens and paper?							
Breakfast organized?							
Lunch packed?							
Snack packed?							
Clothes laid out?							
Alarm set?							
Gas in car?							
Weather conditions?							
Other							

Use various planning and organization methods

Everyone has their own individual methods of planning and organizing for meetings and events such as desk calendars, wall calendars, daily journals, to-do lists, or cell phone notes. Even the method you use today may change with different jobs and work environments. For example, ten years ago, when I worked from one location, I used a desk calendar. Now that I travel around, my calendar is on my smartphone, which I can take with me wherever I go. It is best to stay current with technology and news apps that can help you with planning and organizing.

Tip: Always do the hardest work first.

Prioritize

Discuss with your immediate supervisor which tasks are most important. You may think a certain task is important, but in the big picture, considering all short-term and long-term projects, it may not be. It would benefit you to keep a short- and long-term list. For example, in the morning I pull up my Google calendar for the list of meetings that I need to attend that day, but I also have long-term projects that need to be completed by certain deadlines. Therefore, I have planned for some time each day to work on the larger projects. I break each project down into small segments and then plan to accomplish a small task each day.

Tip: Make a decision to work on your top priorities.

STORY

In order to complete a project like writing this book, I had to discipline myself to write for a half hour a day to finish it! There were days when I was inundated with things to do, so it was important to rank my to-do list and prioritize the workload so I could leave time to write. I made up for days where I just couldn't write at all, by writing for an hour or two to make up for it. My favorite place to write is on airplanes (that's where I am writing this!). It gives me uninterrupted time, with just enough noise to keep me awake, and just enough noise and activity not to distract me. Another place I can write uninterrupted is at my house in the mountains in Mexico!

EXERCISE

PRIORITY LIST

Write in your short-term and long-term priorities in the order of importance to you.

Short-term	Long-term

Manage your time

Employers will expect tasks to be completed in a timely manner because they need a return on the salary they are paying you. Establishing strong time management skills will help you keep track of appointments, tasks, meetings, and deadlines— keeping you on schedule and helping you steer clear of the last-minute rush to complete tasks. Your time management can produce efficiency and save your business a lot of time and money. When time management becomes a routine, you will experience less stress completing tasks and look forward to marking tasks off your schedule. See below for a time management worksheet to help you prioritize.

Tip: Being efficient with your working time allows more free time to enjoy your life outside of work.

STORY

Anne was the master scheduler. She knew that she had difficulties with remembering things, so she kept several calendars and posted notes for every area of life. When Anne would stop in the center to chat, she always appeared to be busy and flustered, and she would say that there were not enough hours in the day to complete her tasks. When discussing the importance of getting an internship or job, the thought of trying to schedule that into her day caused too much stress and anxiety.

It took some coaching for Anne to realize that when you use more than one calendar, it's easy to get them confused. With multiple calendars, you risk double-booking events or missing important appointments. Instead, Anne started to focus on successfully inputting and tracking events, and receiving reminders from one calendar that she kept with her at all times. We suggested she write all of her personal, school, and work reminders on it, including deadline dates, appointments, events, tests, and reminders. When she started utilizing the one calendar, she quickly realized that she was able to manage her time effectively and it reduced her amount of stress. She realized there was a lot of unused time in a single day.

—*Michele Ramsay, Program Director, CIP Brevard*

EXERCISE

WHERE DOES YOUR TIME GO?

STEP 1: RECORD (WRITE DOWN EVERYTHING YOU DO DURING THE DAY)

7:00 AM _____

8:00 AM _____

9:00 AM _____

10:00 AM _____

11:00 AM _____

12:00 PM _____

1:00 PM _____

2:00 PM _____

3:00 PM _____

4:00 PM _____

5:00 PM _____

6:00 PM _____

7:00 PM _____

Where Does Your Time Go? continues

STEP 2: ANALYZE (PICK YOUR FIVE BIGGEST TIME WASTERS, AND ADD UP THE TIME)

Time waster	Amount of time
1.	
2.	
3.	
4.	
5.	

Total: _____ hours   _____ hours

STEP 3: CHANGE (WRITE DOWN THINGS YOU WANT TO SPEND TIME DOING IN ORDER OF IMPORTANCE)

1. _____

2. _____

3. _____

4. _____

5. _____

6. _____

Organize your work space

Less clutter can equate to less stress when trying to complete tasks at work, no matter what kind of work space you use. You may need a visual picture of what a productive workplace setting should resemble. If you are working at a desk, it should only include the necessities: pen, pencil, sticky notes, desk calendar, notepad, stapler, tape, and computer. If you utilize a pantry, kitchen, supply closet, or other physical work space, make sure that similar objects are grouped together, you know where everything is, and you're able to move through the space in an efficient manner. If you work mostly on your computer—a virtual file cabinet—organize your files and projects so that you can quickly pull them up. Again, your organizational method may be personalized to you, but a system needs to be in place for you to be productive.

Call in when you have to miss work

Sometimes we miss work without meaning or wanting to, but you have to call or talk to your supervisor as soon as you know you will miss a day or be late. Talk with your supervisor about their preferences, and follow the guidelines below.

- Ask your supervisor how he/she would prefer you to contact him or her—work phone, cell phone, text, or email—if you are sick or have an emergency.

- Ask what time they would appreciate the contact.

- Program your supervisor's number and the work phone into your cell phone.

- Know that it is never appropriate to just not show up. If you get stranded, ask someone for a phone or ask them to call in for you.

- If you aren't feeling well, call as soon as you know that you will be too sick to go to work.

- Even if you oversleep or don't have a good excuse, call and explain the circumstances.

Tip: Always call in even if you are just going to be late.

STORY

Chris had progressed from an unpaid internship to a paid job working in the kitchen and dining room for a retirement living community. He had received stellar reviews as an intern; however, as soon as he became an employee, everything changed. Suddenly, he was not working fast enough or getting enough done. Chris was feeling stressed and overwhelmed. So we arranged for an occupational therapist (OT) to conduct a job site analysis.

The OT observed Chris at work and made recommendations to help him increase his efficiency. For example, when putting clean items away, instead of carrying just a few items at a time, Chris should load up as many items as possible on a clean tray so that he could reduce the number of trips he had to make. The OT also recommended keeping the cart in front of him to eliminate unnecessary reaching and reduce time. Chris implemented these initial suggestions, but he was still struggling with speed and feared losing his job, so a follow-up analysis was conducted.

Additional recommendations included the following:

- Listen to music to help time go by faster and reduce Chris's stress level.

- Soak the dirty pots and pans while Chris washed the glasses, dishes, and utensils. This will make the pots and pans easier to scrub by hand later.

- Bring carts containing dirty items closer to the sink to save time and simplify his workload.

- Practice sorting silverware at home by spreading out the utensils into a shallow pile and picking them up one type at a time.

By working with an OT, Chris learned that how one sets up and navigates their work space makes a huge difference in work speed and, thus, overall performance.

—*Jennifer Kolarik, Career Coordinator, CIP Brevard*

THE IMPORTANCE OF PLANNING AND ORGANIZING

There's no getting around it: you will need to be able to work on different projects, with different goals and deadlines, at the same time. An unorganized person may get confused, miss a deadline, or do the wrong task at the wrong time. The only solution to being successful and efficient at work is to become an organized person. You have to be determined and want to change old unorganized habits, and your mentors can assist you in making these changes. Planning and organizing will help you develop executive functions such as:

- mental planning (working memory)
- the persistence to complete a task or activity
- keeping track of your belongings and actions
- self-regulating and exhibiting self-control
- self-monitoring your behavior.

Without executive functioning abilities, you might have difficulty with:

- predicting what will happen next at work
- inflexibility/getting stuck/needing to preserve sameness
- attending or concentrating on work
- impulsivity (blurting out)
- managing and allocating time (especially with respect to workday requirements)
- keeping track of belongings/materials; forgetting things you need to bring to work or that you need to do at work
- doing multi-step or complex tasks
- disorganization
- planning.

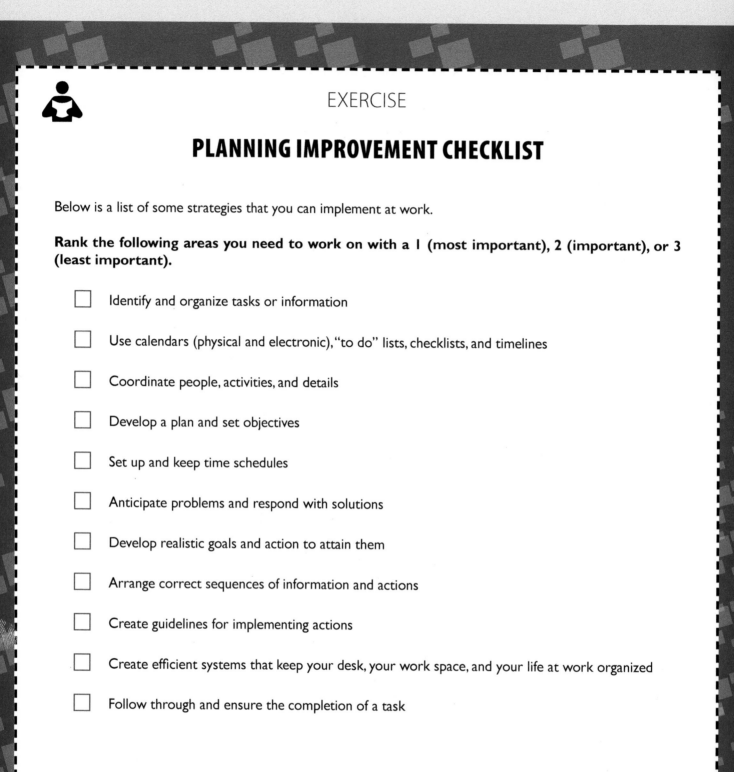

EXERCISE

PLANNING IMPROVEMENT CHECKLIST

Below is a list of some strategies that you can implement at work.

Rank the following areas you need to work on with a 1 (most important), 2 (important), or 3 (least important).

☐   Identify and organize tasks or information

☐   Use calendars (physical and electronic), "to do" lists, checklists, and timelines

☐   Coordinate people, activities, and details

☐   Develop a plan and set objectives

☐   Set up and keep time schedules

☐   Anticipate problems and respond with solutions

☐   Develop realistic goals and action to attain them

☐   Arrange correct sequences of information and actions

☐   Create guidelines for implementing actions

☐   Create efficient systems that keep your desk, your work space, and your life at work organized

☐   Follow through and ensure the completion of a task

DEMONSTRATING EXECUTIVE FUNCTIONING SKILLS TO YOUR EMPLOYER

You can show your abilities in many ways:

- Make short- and long-term goals for job performance.

- Explain how you organized a meeting, task, or event.

- Make a plan for a company volunteer or community service project.

- Create a shared Google calendar for meetings.

- Create a shared Google document for a group project.

- Create a mini-training manual that will show others how you did your job.

Tip: Employers want organized people working for them.

STORY

Josh's employer had a series of positions turn over. He was frustrated in having to constantly retrain employees. There were too many intricacies for each job that took a lot of time and experience on the job to accomplish.

Josh's employer decided to be proactive and gave staff time to fully write up detailed job descriptions that contained exactly how they accomplished their jobs. He reviewed and edited them and handed them back to staff to develop further.

This process took four months and had many benefits. He was able to understand their positions better, had up-to-date job descriptions, and was able to train incoming staff more easily by going through these documents with them.

CHAPTER SIX

Self-Management

*"A self that goes on changing is
a self that goes on living."*

Virginia Woolf[6]

I say the following statement to myself many times a month: "I am responsible for my own emotional happiness." It is very reassuring to know that I don't have to wait for some person or situation to change for me to be happy. As self-change agents, we have the power to alter the way we feel and how we respond to situations in our lives. As my friend Al says, "We are the 'common denominator' in all of our problems, and we are also the solution." Self-soothing and managing your own emotions are necessary to keep balance at work, at school, at home, and in public. We need to look at all the areas that contribute to our being in-balance or out-of-balance, then alter what we are doing and being to produce our desired results.

Tip: Move a muscle, change a thought.

STORY

Growing up, I had no concept of how to take care of myself. Sure I knew how to take a shower, get dressed, clean up my room, and do my chores and homework, but I knew nothing about maintaining a balance in what I ate, how I slept, what exercise I got, and all the "wellness areas" that I now focus on.

As a young man, I got married and had children right away. The stress of working a job, owning a home, and having several small children threw me out of balance. I didn't even realize the sensory issues I had. I never even thought about the effect of certain foods on my behavior or emotional state. I never knew how my sleep patterns affected my meltdowns at work during the middle of the day.

It wasn't until my diagnosis that I started to understand the implications of my actions and began to work on taking care of myself in all these critical areas, building a wellness routine. I started to eat a healthy snack mid-morning at work because I would have low blood sugar and get irritable. I turned off the fluorescent lights in my office and put a soft incandescent lamp at my desk. I exercised for half an hour three times a week (swimming was best). I started eating less fat and sugar and more greens and fruits. All of these things helped me maintain my balance.

STARTING OUT

The first step is being aware of your physical, emotional, and spiritual wellbeing and being able to assess it on a daily basis. Use HALT (Hungry, Angry, Lonely, Tired) to assess yourself.

Here's how to use it: if you have one high area on the scale, let's say Hunger, you can take care of that by, for example, finding a source of protein as soon as possible. If you have two high areas going at the same time, then you may be able to handle that by implementing some quick actions. Let's say, in addition to being very Hungry, you are also very Lonely. You can eat some protein and then call a friend on the way to work or school. If you have three areas going at once, however, that becomes a red flag to stop what you are doing and take care of yourself. If the issues are important enough, you may have to take a self-imposed time-out, take a walk or go outside, and try to deal with a couple of the areas to de-escalate.

If all four areas are at high levels then you need to take immediate action and either take the day off from work or school, seek help in some area, or do several things to bring down the temperature in your boiling pot. Again, emotional happiness is your own responsibility, and you cannot blow up emotionally on others with some unacceptable excuse that if they knew what you were dealing with they would understand.

EXERCISE

PERSONAL HALT CHECKLIST

Make copies of this checklist. Then use them to judge your levels by marking each thermometer with the corresponding values you feel at the moment and discussing your answers with others.

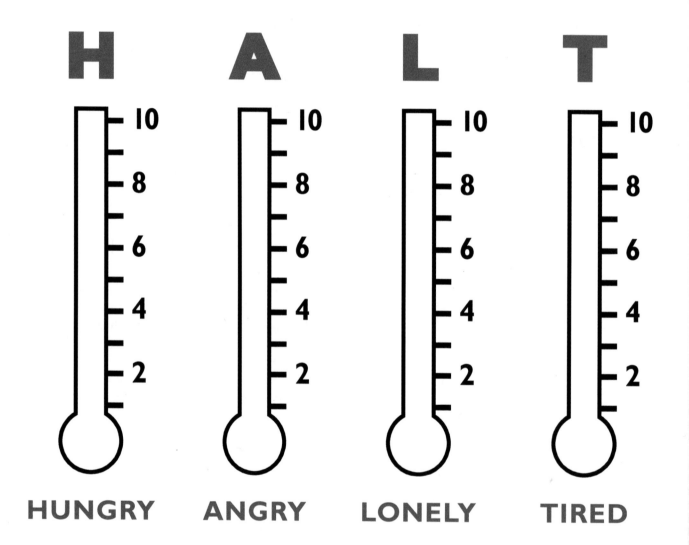

STRESS AT WORK OR SCHOOL

It is necessary to leave your problems at the door when you enter work or school. At work, for instance, your employer is paying for you to be present and work on their goals, and you must concentrate on your work and relate to others in a proactive manner. Everyone wants their work and school environment to be calm, enjoyable, and productive. Problem people are like squeaky wheels, and they have no support among the staff or students. They become isolated and are the first to be let go.

An outburst or overreaction can ruin your chances for success, so you should use the preventive strategies throughout this chapter to avoid meltdowns at work and keep problems at bay. Of course, a certain number of issues will arise even if you have taken care of yourself. These will be tests of your ability to self-manage your stress or anxiety.

Tip: Use restraint of tongue and text.

STORY

Mary, a student who was diagnosed with Asperger's, Obsessive Compulsive Disorder, and anxiety, faced formidable obstacles securing and retaining employment. The primary issue Mary faced was becoming so focused on a task that she had difficulty moving past it. She would get so stressed out that she became paralyzed.

Mary discussed her issues and possible coping strategies in career counseling. CIP always stresses that if students are cognizant and accepting of their diagnosis first, then they can make progress in all areas. Since Mary was accepting of her diagnosis, we were able to brainstorm and come up with ways for her to self-manage her stress and anxiety in the workplace.

We decided that developing good eating habits and exercising on a regular basis would give Mary a good foundation in neutralizing the stress she felt from her heavy schedule and internships. We also determined that breaking her tasks into segments and setting time limits would prevent her from spending too much time doing one task and ignoring others. Rather than let a concern distract her or prevent her from moving forward on the task at hand, Mary began jotting down her questions as they occurred, but kept on working. She would then ask her supervisor her questions when she had a chance. After developing these coping strategies, Mary successfully completed internships at a clothing department store and at the Humane Society, caring for animals that she loves so much!

—*Shannon Miller, Career Coordinator, CIP Berkshire*

STRESS AT HOME

Your spouse or roommate(s) will want the same as an employer: an atmosphere of peace, calm, and mutual respect. Meshing the lifestyles of two or more individuals from very different backgrounds and with different expectations can often bring about stress that can spill over into the workplace if not managed. You need to problem-solve in a rational manner without anxiety or fearful reaction, and you may need to use new skills that you have not learned before, such as negotiation and compromise.

STORY

Candice learned about managing stress at home when living with several college roommates. Although she would make good plans to accomplish what she needed to do for her course assignments, she often became consumed with her roommate frustrations and she began to miss deadlines. She then struggled to get out of bed each day, fell further behind in her schoolwork, and felt more stress and despair.

Candice's frustrations stemmed mainly from her expectations regarding her roommates, rather than any one particular roommate issue. For example, if they were being loud or doing something that interfered with her studying, she would feel aggravated that they were not changing their approach, rather than considering adapting her own ways by going to campus, the library, or another quiet place to study, wearing headphones to block out the noise, or negotiating with them for quiet time. She was also frustrated because she thought they were not progressing in their life goals as fast as she was progressing or as fast as she thought they should progress.

While dealing with roommates is still a daily challenge for Candice, she developed strategies to help her in this arena. First, she takes responsibility for identifying a quiet place to study when needed. Also, she takes steps to manage her overall wellness and emotional regulation. When she feels her frustrations rising, she takes a walk; she eats regular healthy meals, rather than binging periodically on junk food. And if she finds herself getting behind in any assignments, she calls or emails her academic advisor. She reaches out to her roommates in a positive way, rather than just turning inward in an unhealthy way or lashing out at them. And because she has worked really hard on managing the stress she feels at home, Candice will soon complete her Bachelor's degree, a long-term goal of hers.

—*Jennifer Kolarik, Career Coordinator, CIP Brevard*

HOW TO MANAGE STRESS

When you feel overwhelmed, you lose confidence and may become irritable or withdrawn. This can make you less productive and less effective and make school or work seem less rewarding. If you ignore the warning signs of stress, they can lead to a bigger problem. During the course of an ordinary day you might:

- feel anxious, irritable, or depressed

- feel apathetic or have a loss of interest in what you are doing

- feel tired or sleepy

- have trouble concentrating

- experience muscle tension or headaches

- have stomach problems

- use alcohol or drugs as a coping mechanism.

You can't control everything at home, school, or in your work environment, but that doesn't mean that you're powerless—even when you're stuck in a difficult situation. Finding ways to manage stress isn't about making huge changes, moving to a new apartment, or rethinking career ambitions, but rather about focusing on the one thing that you can control: you! When your needs are taken care of, you're stronger and more resilient to stress. The better you feel, the better equipped you'll be to manage stress without becoming overwhelmed. Below are many proactive steps you can take that will help with your self-management and emotional regulation.

Tip: To alleviate stress, make sure to balance work with fun. What are the fun things you can do in your free time to alleviate stress? DO THEM!

TIPS FOR PRACTICE

Get regular exercise

It's a powerful stress reliever—even though it may be the last thing you feel like doing. Any activity that raises your heart rate and makes you sweat is an effective way to lift your mood, increase energy, sharpen focus, and relax your mind, body, and spirit. Even walking around the building or grounds mid-morning or mid-afternoon to get some air helps to relieve stress.

> *Tip: Even 20 minutes of some kind of exercise two or three times a week has proven highly beneficial to one's health.*

Make good food choices

Making good food choices that give you energy and keep you going can help you get through stressful events and help you avoid mood swings. Eat whole natural proteins and vegetables, and limit your intake of caffeine, sugary fruit juices, and sodas.

> *Tip: Keep healthy snacks around so that you can grab one on the move.*

Get enough sleep

Not only can stress and worry create insomnia, but lack of sleep can leave you vulnerable to even more stress. When you are well rested, it's much easier to keep your emotional balance, so that you can cope with stress in relationships and in the workplace. To improve the quantity and quality of your sleep time, have a plan on how you can relax at night. Avoid caffeine and high-sugared foods in the evening. Try a period of quiet meditation before bed. Unplug from your devices (computer, tablet, TV, cell phone, etc.).

> *Tip: "Early to bed, early to rise, makes a man healthy, wealthy, and wise."*

Get up a little earlier

Rise a little earlier to make room in your schedule. Be able to go slow or sit down on the porch with your coffee and watch the sun coming up or the birds fly around. Even ten minutes can make a difference between frantically rushing to work compared to having time to ease into your day.

> *Tip: Each evening organize your work clothing, prepare lunch, and pack snacks and drinks for the next day.*

STORY

Over the years, I have developed a morning routine that helps me start the day peacefully.

When I awaken I usually say a prayer of thanksgiving. I may stay in bed for a while and say this slowly and attempt to calm myself before rushing out of bed and into life. I may slip out of bed onto my knees and continue a short prayer. After taking care of necessities, I light a candle and use only that light to operate with. This creates a peaceful ambience to quietly move around the kitchen. I let the dogs outside to do their business and then let them in.

I prepare a glass of hot green tea and sit down at the kitchen table and put my hands around the glass to warm them and center myself. I open a meditation book and read a short reading. I then sit and try to meditate on the reading, while accepting all the noises of the dogs, traffic, or any other movement, just letting those noises and the thoughts they produce pass by me. I will sip the tea and maybe eat some cereal quietly and set my intention for the day. Some days this is effective, and some days I am totally or partially distracted and the meditation is disrupted.

The goal is to try to take this centering state with me throughout my interactions during the day. Some days I will remember my intention the whole day and try to act on it. Other days life blasts in and I sort of unconsciously wander through the day without living intentionally, maybe caught up in fear or reaction. I can always return to my intention and state of peace just by thinking so and being calm.

Part of this regime is to also swim three mornings a week, take at least one or two walks a day with the dogs, and eat mindfully the quantity and quality of foods that will nourish my body and keep me self-aware.

I end the day in a calm manner and do what is necessary to relax and prepare for a good night's sleep. I nourish my spirit by reading or watching something that will encourage positive relationships and reach out to others, and I review my actions for a short time to help set the intention for the next day. To relax, I sometimes imagine myself lying on a blanket on the sand on a warm sunny beach and let my body sink into it. I also sometimes imagine two very large hands that I can lay in; for me they are the hands of God to protect me and keep me safe.

Have a balanced schedule

Analyze your schedule with your supervisor to ensure it is balanced. Look at your daily responsibilities and tasks and, if needed, ask for accommodations. All work and no play is a recipe for burnout. Try to find a balance between work, family life, social activities, solitary pursuits, your daily responsibilities, and just plain down time. Build in breaks and prioritize your work so you feel balanced and productive.

> *Tip: Take a break or a walk outside after finishing a long report.*

Limit over-commitments

Avoid over-scheduling things back-to-back or trying to fit too much into one day. If you are feeling over-committed, then find some things you can let go of, delegate work to others, or ask for help so that you do not feel as overwhelmed. Distinguish between the "should" and the "must." Drop tasks that aren't truly necessary to the bottom of your list or eliminate them entirely.

> *Tip: It's better to do three things well than to do six things poorly.*

Organize your living and work space

Change the furniture around to gain a new perspective. Organize your living space so it is convenient for you. Set up a quiet area for meditation, yoga, or reading. Do the same at work. Organize your work space to promote productivity and comfort (e.g., purchase a supportive office chair). Make your environment work for you.

> *Tip: Add some color or a plant to your work space. Change things up when you get bored.*

Reduce clutter

Take a few minutes each day to organize a small area of your office, car, home, or desk. Clean out one drawer or cabinet at a time and make items more accessible. Get rid of junk or things that are in the way. Doing a little each day to organize your belongings adds up over a few days and you feel a real sense of relief.

> *Tip: Spend five minutes per day putting things away or cleaning up one small table or area.*

Plan regular breaks (not breakdowns)

Plan small breaks at work (either alone or with others). Stepping away can briefly relax you and allow you to refocus and be more productive. Even short breaks to take a walk or sit back and clear your mind help. Also plan days off or small vacations; even time at home can be used to catch up on hobbies or projects.

> *Tip: Try to eat lunch in another environment. Take your food to the lounge or outside picnic table.*

Resist perfectionism

Perfectionism is the killer of all great ideas and projects. Persistence is one thing, but perfectionism is deadly. Accepting that the outcome will not be exactly as you planned will take a lot of stress off you. No project, situation, or decision is ever perfect, so set realistic goals, be willing to restart, revise, and move forward, and expect that things will not go exactly as planned. Give yourself permission to be imperfect. There is a saying: there are no mistakes, only approximations to the right answer. So keep trying new things and keep refining your skills.

> *Tip: If you are a person who must complete one thing before moving on to another, leave a project half-complete and do something else for a while, then come back and complete it later or the next day.*

Don't try to control the uncontrollable

Life is constantly changing and each moment we are transitioning to the next. When we accept that and get into the flow of it, life is so much easier. People do unexpected and foolish things that make no sense to us, and we need to accept that we cannot control the

outcome of most things in our lives. Acceptance is a much happier way to live. It doesn't mean accepting bad things and not trying to take action about them; it means accepting the reality in front of us and then moving forward as best we can.

> *Tip: When life throws you a lemon, make lemonade—lots of lemonade!*

Flip negative thinking

Make a conscious choice to think positive. Find the silver lining of every situation: what worked correctly and what you enjoy. Life doesn't get any better than it is at this moment, and if you are not happy on a daily basis, you won't be happy even if **everything in your life is working well**. Waiting for happiness is a waste of the *now*—and why not enjoy life *now*? Try to think positively regarding your co-workers and reinforce yourself for your own accomplishments, even if no one else does.

> *Tip: Carry around a "Think Positive" stone in your pocket, or put it on your desk at work or in front of your sink at home.*

STORY

In 2006, I was walking down the street in Berkeley, California, frustrated and somewhat down. Trying to start a center, find a building, negotiate a lease, interview staff, order phone service, and complete the myriad of other tasks was overwhelming me. I was saying negative things to myself, and finally I said, "Michael, you need to Think Positive." At that same moment my eyes turned toward a store windowsill and perched there was a stone that had written on it "Think Positive." I felt a little guilty taking it, but put the stone in my pocket anyway. I felt the stone every time I put my hand in my pocket. At night I put it on the nightstand in the hotel. It got me through a rough time struggling to accomplish my complicated work alone, and was a physical presence and reminder to stay positive. I found a source of similar stones near the bay and got a marker and made several more. I placed one at the original spot that I picked up the first stone and left several in many other places, such as bathroom counters and restaurant tables.

I now repurpose many of these rocks, bringing "Think Positive" stones to many conferences and speaking engagements all over the U.S. and internationally. Most people just enjoy keeping them on their desk, in their purse, or in their pocket.

Over the years I have had people tell me wonderful stories regarding the effect of having the stones. One person from Switzerland said her brother's wife had cancer and that her brother had asked her the day before getting the stone to "think positive thoughts" for him and his wife. They both got stones.

Make good decisions for yourself

Value yourself enough to do the right things that make sense for you. Take your time and make the right decision. Think things through. Use your mentors and the Donkey Rule (see the "Problem Solving and Critical Thinking" chapter earlier) to make good decisions. You have a right to be happy and relaxed and to make decisions in the time that makes sense for you.

> Tip: Take your time making important decisions (poll your mentors!).

Spend time with friends and at social outlets

"No man is an island," and we do not exist in a vacuum. We are a social species, and if we get isolated and depressed we need to take action to change that. Go to a great movie, arrange to meet a friend for coffee, or play a sport with friends. Don't just sit there; do something to help yourself. If you ignore this one, you will not only be less productive but also less happy in your daily life.

> Tip: Make a vow to yourself that, when others invite you to an event, you say "Yes" unless you absolutely can't go for some very important reason.

EXERCISE

YOUR SELF-MANAGEMENT PLAN

GETTING EXERCISE:

How? _____

When? _____

MAKING GOOD FOOD CHOICES:

What? _____

GETTING ENOUGH SLEEP:

When? _____

A BALANCED WORK SCHEDULE:

When? _____

LIMIT OVER-COMMITMENTS:

How? _____

ORGANIZE YOUR LIVING AREA AND WORK SPACE:

How? _____

When? _____

REDUCE CLUTTER:

Where? _____

Your Self-Management Plan continues

GET UP A LITTLE EARLIER:

When? _____

PLAN REGULAR BREAKS:

When? _____

RESIST PERFECTIONISM:

How? _____

DON'T TRY TO CONTROL THE UNCONTROLLABLE:

How? _____

FLIP NEGATIVE THINKING:

How? _____

MAKE GOOD DECISIONS FOR YOURSELF:

What? _____

SPEND TIME WITH FRIENDS AND AT SOCIAL OUTLETS:

When? _____

CHAPTER SEVEN

Willingness to Learn

HOW TO DEVELOP YOUR WILLINGNESS TO LEARN

Employers do not want perfect employees. Instead, they are searching for individuals who have a desire to continually learn, and to continually strive to do better.

"A life spent in making mistakes is not only more honorable but more useful than a life spent in doing nothing."

George Bernard Shaw[7]

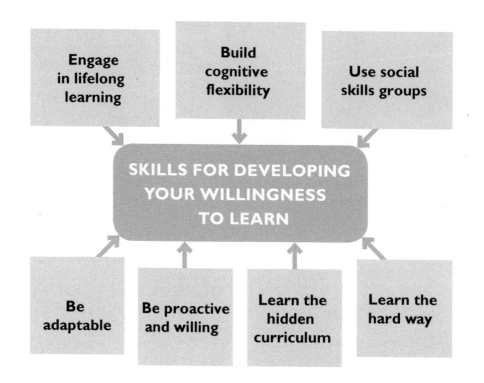

TIPS FOR PRACTICE

Engage in lifelong learning

Lifelong learning is the ongoing, voluntary, and self-motivated pursuit of knowledge for either personal or professional reasons. Therefore, it enhances not only social inclusion, active citizenship, and personal development, but also self-sustainability, competitiveness, and employability. Always be interested in improving yourself, learning new information and skills, and going to extra training that is offered. Each certificate you obtain adds to your résumé and your value as an employee.

Build cognitive flexibility

Many students on the spectrum really resist change. Is it fear? Is it ego? Is it pride? We encourage you to be open to new topics and experiences. Your life experience is like a diamond, and the more you explore its many facets, the more you shine. No matter your age, you learn a bit more each day about who you are and how the world around you works. This allows you to test your potential, leading to the most important parts of the evolutionary path: self-discovery and self-confidence.

As you grow and develop, you reach certain critical points in your life where you are challenged beyond your resistance (beyond what you think you are capable of responding to), but new topics and experiences are what move you forward. Growth is as simple as mastering a willingness to learn new ideas and new ways of thinking. There is much out there that you do not know, but if you can learn to grow and discover, you may find exactly what you need to help boost your confidence to a point where you feel like you can achieve anything, leading to successful breakthroughs. When you open up, you start seeing yourself as part of the real world, instead of a separate piece some distance from it.

Knowledge of the self is a confidence builder, but sometimes you hit a wall and all you want to do is retreat to your dorm room and sleep it off, or distract yourself with video games and movies. It is not always easy, but the goal should be to identify the places where you become resistant and move from one mentality to another.

STORY

Marcus enjoys the Internet. He loves looking up new and unusual topics on his phone related to science, history, politics, and anthropology. He also enjoys playing a few games or two when he has the free time. Marcus is onto something. He has an openness and willingness to learn from the topics and links that he clicks. He is willing to read any article (as long as it comes from a credible source). What Marcus takes from his reading is stored in his brain, mixing with the other concepts and ideas that he has absorbed over the years. When Marcus speaks, he infuses his conversations with the information he has learned through his studies. His ideas may not always flow or develop naturally within the conversation, but they are, nonetheless, thought-provoking. "But what good is this?" one may ask. "How does this help Marcus at his internship, or what about those classes he's taking that aren't even related to what he reads online?"

Marcus has an advantage. By just being passionate about something, he is able to transfer his willingness to learn into those topics that may not interest him. Marcus has a valuable tool in his collective learning toolbox. He can use this self-motivating attitude to propel him through his late-night papers and early-morning exams.

The academic support staff love working with Marcus because they know just what it takes to keep him on track. They are able to remind Marcus about applying his willingness to learn during those times he's not as passionate about what he's studying, and it works wonderfully for

him. Each day that goes by, Marcus is becoming more receptive to learning new things as he meets those deadlines for his current classes. Marcus still needs a lot of support, but he arrives to work with support staff with a willingness to learn and a winning attitude.

—*Charles Culp, Career Coordinator, CIP Bloomington*

Use social skills groups

It's important for you to work hard and push forward into new realms of thought. You can do this by cultivating challenging experiences and conversations with others in the diverse community around you. We encourage you to seek and interact with passionate people who have mastered a given craft. Glass blowers, video game designers, and transcendental meditation teachers can best relate their occupations to you directly. Listening to speakers such as these in a social skills group can be highly beneficial. When you get a chance to discuss any topic with an expert in the field, you come away with a new sense of the true potential that exists within yourself.

> *Tip: Join a social group to increase your ability to socialize with others.*

Be adaptable

Good employees are able to adapt or mold to the work environment and job at hand. It is especially important for you to learn to adapt to the organizational culture. It is also important for you to be flexible and willing to work with individuals from a wide range of cultures, genders, races, ethnicity, and ages.

> *Tip: In your first month on the job you must be an observer of the "office culture" and mimic how people interact with each other, how they take their breaks, when they eat lunch, how they dress, how they answer the phone, etc.*

STORY

Mohammed was a devoted Muslim student from Saudi Arabia, and Jules was a French-speaking devoted Christian student from Algeria. They both were interning at a Mediterranean restaurant near their college.

Mohammed was put on the schedule to work Friday evenings, and Jules was put on the schedule to work Sunday brunch. Mohammed wanted to be at the Mosque for Friday prayers, and Jules wanted to attend Sunday morning Mass. When they looked at the schedule Jules suggested that they switch shifts and explain this to the supervisor. Two students from very different cultural backgrounds came together to find a solution that worked for everyone.

Be proactive in learning the ropes

When first starting a job, most employers will only teach new employees the basics regarding what they need to know to perform their job properly. However, to excel in a position, employees need to learn about the organization as a whole, the role of other departments, and more advanced aspects of the job.

Some employees request a mentor or just ask another employee to show them the ropes. Some companies offer training opportunities and conferences that employees can attend during work time or on their own. Often these are free. You should take advantage of these whenever they are offered. Any additional skills and knowledge you gain in related areas to your employment are going to make you a more valuable employee.

Tip: Take advantage of training and programs that will improve your worth as an employee.

STORY

Maggie started a job at a large law firm. She enjoyed her job, but she had to do a lot of data entry, which she found very boring. She recognized that if she wanted to advance to other areas of work at her company, she would need to gain proficiency in other skills. She asked her employer what she could do to move up.

It turned out that the company offered customer service training on Thursday evenings for employees who wanted to move to the front of the house and deal with clients. Maggie attended training every week and, at her employer's recommendation, took a law class at the local community college. After one semester she was able to apply for a receptionist position where she was able to work with clients more directly, feel more challenged, and earn a higher salary.

Learn the hidden curriculum

There are many things that need to be learned in the workplace that are unofficial or "unwritten rules." Identifying a co-worker or supervisor who is willing to show you the ropes and give tips on how to avoid sticky situations is really beneficial. That can be a great way to learn about the hidden curriculum of your employment site.

Tip: If you don't know what the dress code is at your work site for the holiday party, ask someone.

Learn the hard way

Sometimes, unfortunately, we have to learn something the long way or the hard way. It's never fun—but it's often necessary and many times results in the most growth. It is also helpful to be willing to learn from those who have already learned a lesson the hard way and can help save you from a potentially painful experience. Why re-invent the wheel (unless it is broken)?

> *Tip: You can learn from more experienced people how to avoid making big mistakes on the job.*

STORY

Sometimes learning the hard way might be what it takes to grow professionally. One student, James, loved working with animals. He was looking forward to interning for the local zoo and sharing his knowledge and love of animals with patrons. The zoo requires that all interns and volunteers go through an orientation, mandatory classes, and then an interview. During orientation, there was a team-based scavenger hunt, and James expressed that he did not want to do it. When he did participate, he corrected volunteers and even the zookeepers, believing that he was right and they were incorrect in their knowledge. He even grabbed the clipboard right out of someone's hands. When they asked him to do something, he came across as argumentative.

Unfortunately James did not realize the impression he was creating during the orientation. He was argumentative, inflexible, and not a team player, so he did not make it to the interview stage. As disappointing as this experience was for James, he learned just how he was coming across—something he truly did not understand before. His difficulty with understanding how others perceived him was preventing him from being successful.

After his experience at the zoo, James started another internship working with animals, but he promptly received similar feedback from his supervisor as he did at the zoo. This feedback helped him realize that he needed to drastically change his approach and quickly! He showed up the next day for his new internship with a completely new attitude, and he even stepped up his dress and hygiene that day, demonstrating that he wanted to succeed!

—*Jennifer Kolarik, Career Coordinator, CIP Brevard*

CHAPTER EIGHT

Technological Proficiency

"From phones to cars to medicine, technology touches every part of our lives. If you can create technology, you can change the world."

Susan Wojcicki, YouTube CEO[8]

Technology is our main way of doing business on the planet. Your technology skills are critical in most employment. Anytime you can increase your knowledge of specific software or applications, you can improve your value to an employer.

STORY

Brian had an internship at an organic farm for a year while he was a student at a local college. He worked in a wide variety of areas, including feeding, watering, and caring for the animals, egg cleaning and packaging, and propagation. He expressed his interest in inventory and operating the cash register to his job coach. The farmer agreed to start training him and, if he did well, to hire him to work the next full season at the register in a paid position. The farmer was switching over his store to operate using an iPad and the "Square" credit-card payment app. For three days on the job, Brian created all the categories on the square and put all the prices in for the entire store inventory. Because of this technological proficiency, Brian was hired to operate the store for the entire season.

USE TECHNOLOGY TO YOUR ADVANTAGE

→ Read Company Websites

→ Use Social Media Skills

→ Avoid Screen Addiction and Technology Abuse

READ COMPANY WEBSITES

Most businesses now have a website. Before you consider a work position, read the company's website and try to understand as much as possible about the business. First, it will let you know whether the work seems right for you. Second, if you make it to the interview stage, then having a working knowledge of the business and website lets the future employer know that you really care about the job and understand what the goals of the company are.

STORY

Pam graduated with a degree in social work and wanted to apply for a position as a caseworker. She found an advertisement for a case manager job at a social welfare agency in the local newspaper. She went online and read the website, discovering that the agency worked with addiction and alcohol issues. Pam had no training or interest in this area, so she checked other ads in the local *Penny Saver* and found one that was for a case manager working with a children's agency. She went online and read the website, and this private agency not only was doing the work she wanted to do but was also a religious organization that was in tune with her values and faith. Pam called and had a preliminary phone interview with the Human Resources Director. They had a discussion regarding her background and the agency's mission. Pam expressed that this was a position that she was very interested in and that it would fit with her values, and explained why she went into this field.

At the scheduled interview, Pam was able to talk about the goals of the agency and how she would fit in with their mission. She had looked at the profile of the Executive Director who was interviewing her and knew about her background and experience. She also found out that the Executive Director had attended the same university she had. All of this preparation helped Pam to secure this position.

USE YOUR SOCIAL MEDIA SKILLS

Social media plays an enormous role in the operations and marketing of businesses of all kinds and sizes. People are doing more work and communication online, letting customers know about events, prices, sales, and other information constantly. Many businesses are trying to cultivate a strong social media presence as a marketing tool and to drive traffic to their websites. Online sales are grabbing a large share of the market, and many businesses are hiring individuals to coordinate their online and social media presence. As a young adult, you probably already have proficiency in these areas. Be sure to mention them on your résumé and during interviews.

STORY

Kate had a certificate from a community college in computer graphics but was unable to complete her two-year degree due to her difficulty passing out of the math modules. She had a year of interning at a computer graphics and design firm doing basic business ads and some website design, and she was connected well on social media, constantly in communication on Facebook, Twitter, Instagram, and Snapchat (though she was careful not to be online for personal reasons during her work time).

When a Marketing Assistant position opened up at the firm she had interned at, she applied. The company was interested in hiring someone who could maintain an online presence, update their Facebook page, list events on other sites, promote new products, and answer online inquiries. Kate was really good at all of these areas and was able to explain this during the interview and procure the position.

AVOID SCREEN ADDICTION AND TECHNOLOGY ABUSE

What you do in your own time is up to you. How you spend your time at work is not. Time is money, and if you are spending a significant portion of your time at work on your own phone or on social media, then you are, in effect, stealing time from your employer. Moreover, most employers can now see where you are spending your time through their IT department and you can be fired for doing it.

If you are using the business email to explore illicit sites then you can bring a virus into the system and create havoc with the server. You also can overload the server with videos, games, and other content, which can cause problems for the business. If you want to check your email or text with friends, you need to do it during breaks or lunchtime. Surfing the Internet for personal reasons limits your chances of success on the job because you are spending time off task and not contributing to the business.

MANAGING PERSONAL SCREEN TIME AT WORK

- Turn your cell phone off or turn the volume to mute at work. Don't spend your work time surfing the Internet.

- Limit personal cell phone calls and texts at work.

- Follow the office or work policies regarding phone and Internet usage.

- Avoid websites that will introduce possible viruses into the computer network.

- Protect your computer password and report any security issues that occur.

- Delete all unneeded email on a regular basis.

- Only include people who need to be on an email and do not share any vital or highly sensitive information by email or text. Do that "face-to-face" to avoid miscommunication and misunderstandings.

- Keep your voicemail box clear so that you can receive important messages.

- Make sure the email content you are sharing is appropriate. Refrain from sending political, religious, or humorous content, or complaints. Avoid commenting on "office politics."

- Don't let personal phone calls disrupt the office or get in the way of doing business and do not play voicemail out loud.

- Set your social media setting to private.

In short, you should refrain from researching any content that does not relate to work. The misuse of computer time at work is grounds for dismissal. If you feel that you have a problem controlling your use of screens then you should seek professional help outside of work, or go to your company's Human Resources Department for assistance.

STORY

Ron was diagnosed in high school with Asperger's Syndrome and anxiety. When he arrived at CIP, we didn't know that he also had issues around electronic overuse. Ron isolated himself from all his classes and appointments and could not self-limit his electronic usage. Ron was most comfortable with himself when he was connected online. Having online relationships with people who did not know his challenges or diagnosis felt safer and less anxiety-provoking.

We wanted to provide Ron with opportunities to be successful, but we knew that if his electronics were taken completely away he could not cope with the outside world, where we are surrounded by technology and electronics for everyday use in the workplace, at school, and in our personal life. Instead, an individual with electronic overuse issues needs to learn how to self-modulate and create a life balance.

We negotiated several strategies that he agreed to implement. Ron decided to hand in all his electronics at a designated time to a staff member in order for him to get to bed at a decent hour, and he rewarded himself with additional time on his electronics when he attended classes and appointments. For example, if he completed five of his scheduled appointments over the period of three days, he could use his computer or tablet for two hours during the day. If his room was clean and he cooked a proper meal for his roommates, he could use his electronics for an additional hour at night. Ron was able to work towards his goal of being independent and develop the strategies needed by working in alliance with his advisor, career coordinator, and residential staff.

Ron slowly was able to self-manage his electronics and become a productive student and roommate. He managed his priorities and successfully earned a Certified Nursing Assistant (CNA) certificate. His interests around helping others in need helped him to get an internship at a local nursing home under the supervision of the Activities Director. His job responsibilities and time at the nursing home will help him continue to work towards a paid position as a CNA. He currently works a part-time job at a supermarket, has an apartment that he shares with a roommate, and is participating in a local social group.

—*Shannon Miller, Career Coordinator, CIP Berkshire*

PART III

The Employment Toolkit

CHAPTER ONE

Making a Career and Ability Portfolio

Now that you know what your interests and transferable skills are, as well as the eight skills employers are looking for, you can work on making a career portfolio. A portfolio is a type of work sample—a visual way of showing what you are capable of. It's a collection of artifacts and materials that represent work-related events in your life and provides evidence of your potential work ability by showing what you have accomplished. It reconstructs your abilities, skills, achievements, and accomplishments.

A career portfolio does not replace a résumé but augments it. The portfolio is usually presented during an interview, not sent out with your résumé. Its purpose is to show that you can do the job by demonstrating that you have completed the tasks in the portfolio. It is never too soon to start building a career portfolio online or in a folder (or both).

A career and ability portfolio will help you:

- prepare for interviews

- convince others of your skills, abilities, and qualities

- communicate clearly and help you guide your interview conversation

- showcase your skills

- demonstrate the results of your work

- document your accomplishments

- assess your progress in your career development

- make clear your work preferences and learning style.

Before presenting a career portfolio to an employer, research examples of various formats a portfolio can take. Employers are interested in seeing your skills, abilities, experience, and personal qualities that relate specifically to the work they need done, so you need to tailor or customize your portfolio differently for each job interview.

STORY

Temple Grandin, a woman with Asperger's Syndrome, has had movies made and books written about her. She studied cattle processing plants and came up with her own design that was more efficient, kosher, and saved the lives of many cattle—but she had a hard time getting anyone to listen to her because of her odd social qualities. In the movie *Temple Grandin* there is a scene when she is trying to explain her idea to several cattle processing plant supervisors. She cannot get their attention at all, so she pulls out her design portfolio, and once she has their attention on the drawings, she is able to sell them on the efficiency of her designs (a picture is worth a thousand words!). Without this portfolio, she never would have gotten the job, and now cattle processing plants around the world are built using her designs.

WHAT GOES IN A CAREER AND ABILITY PORTFOLIO?

An artifact is any tangible object or item that can represent your accomplishments or qualities. Artifacts include:

- certificates of achievement or completion

- work samples (things you have created or made)

  - artwork, writing samples, photographs, reports, research, computer print-outs, graphics, handouts, published articles, invitations, programs, brochures, fliers, or newsletters

- letters of recommendation

- work or school evaluations

- photographs of yourself on the job site or accepting an award

- video clips of you at work or making a presentation

  - articles written about you

  - awards you've received

  - a statement of your idea or philosophy

(For example, this is what Temple Grandin did when she drew her plans for a cattle processing plant. She made a series of sketches that portrayed the system she had in mind that would process cattle in a more humane way.)

- things you've created to summarize or represent things you have done.

(For example, a summary of evaluations from a workshop you gave, achievements from a career-specific training course that you took (like CPR), or a chart showing contributions you made to a project.)

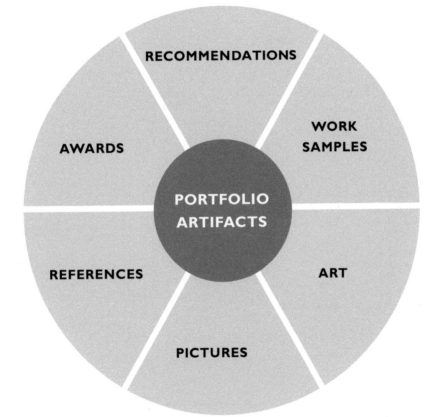

PORTFOLIO DEVELOPMENT CHECKLIST

Use a professional binder or accordion file. Use clean copies, rather than originals. Organize by categories with separation dividers. Label each artifact with a name. Use graphics and color as much as possible.

Artifact: **Which talent/ability/skill it highlights:**

☐ Certificates received   _____

☐ Letters of recommendation   _____

☐ Work or school evaluations   _____

☐ College transcripts   _____

☐ Photos of you at work   _____

☐ Video clips   _____

☐ Articles written about you   _____

☐ Awards/achievements   _____

☐ Statement of idea/philosophy _____

☐ Summary of work   _____

☐ Work samples   _____

☐ _____ _____

☐ _____ _____

☐ _____ _____

CHAPTER TWO

Developing a Résumé

A résumé is a document that lists your name and contact information; education; work, internship, and volunteer experience; and any special skills you have. Potential employers will ask applicants to submit a résumé so they can screen candidates for the required skills, experiences, and abilities needed for a specific job opening. They will scan your résumé and compare it to the others they receive, and invite the most qualified candidates for an interview. Developing a good résumé is one of the most important things you can do as you prepare for the world of work. Its purpose is to highlight your skills and get you to the interview stage of the job search. In addition to a print résumé, you will need to develop an electronic résumé that uses keywords to generate as many hits as possible by résumé search software. Emphasize nouns (sought by search software) and save in the format required by the employer (.doc, .pdf, etc.). A web résumé can also include professional graphics, video clips, photographs, etc. that a traditional résumé does not capture. If you do not have a résumé, you will not get an interview for most jobs. Prospective employers at job fairs will not be willing to speak with you about your skills and work experience.

You will also need at least three professional references during your job search process, for example a professor, previous supervisor, or job coach. These people may be called and asked questions about the quality of your work, how you work with others, or how you handle stress or pressure.

SOME THINGS TO REMEMBER

- If you are applying for a highly competitive job, your résumé will need to focus on your accomplishments.

- For an entry-level position, you should highlight your strengths, schoolwork, activities, achievements, and relevant work experience.

- Be truthful about the work, time spent, and duties on previous jobs.

- Demonstrate through real examples why you are the best person for the job.

- Create a professional, tailored document by keeping the format clean, clear, and easy to read.

- Have three people read your résumé and give you feedback before submitting it to an employer, and make the changes they recommend.

- Use key words such as initiative, dynamic, team player, and self-motivated.

- Use action verbs in describing your work: led, achieved, completed, coordinated, delivered, presented, resolved, organized, etc.

- Remember to get prior approval and the contact information for your professional references.

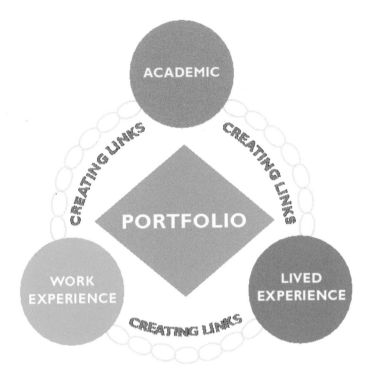

SAMPLE RÉSUMÉ

Margaret Jones

5823 Bounty Lane
Springfield, IL 23587
(516) 286-3490
margaretjones@cip.org

Job Objective

Seeking entry-level receptionist position

Education

Springfield High School, Springfield, IL
Graduation expected June 2017

Relevant Courses

- Office Systems, Keyboarding, Computer Applications, Record-keeping

Skills and Abilities

Office Machines

- Ten-key adding machine

- Word processing (45 WPM)

- Photocopier and fax machine

Computer Skills

- PC: Windows 10, Word, Excel, and PowerPoint

- Macintosh: Microsoft Works

People Skills

- Office aide at Springfield High School in the main office for two semesters

- Organized student fundraisers for Polynesian Club

- Read to, and played checkers with, elderly at nursing home

Hobbies and Interests

- Enjoy reading, drawing, exercising, and hiking with friends

References Furnished Upon Request

EXERCISE

RÉSUMÉ WORKSHEET

CONTACT INFORMATION

Name _____

Address _____

_____

Telephone Number _____

Email Address _____

EDUCATION

Name of School _____

City, State _____

Degree _____

Relevant Courses _____

Dates Attended _____

Name of School _____

City, State _____

Degree _____

Relevant Courses _____

Dates Attended _____

Résumé Worksheet continues

EXPERIENCE

Name of Company _____

City, State _____

Job Title _____

Job Duties _____

Dates Employed _____

Name of Company _____

City, State _____

Job Title _____

Job Duties _____

Dates Employed _____

Name of Company _____

City, State _____

Job Title _____

Job Duties _____

Dates Employed _____

INTERNSHIP EXPERIENCE

Name of Company or Organization _____

City, State _____

Job Title _____

Dates Employed _____

Name of Company or Organization _____

City, State _____

Job Title _____

Dates Employed _____

Résumé Worksheet continues

VOLUNTEER WORK

Name of Organization _____

City, State _____

Type of Work _____

Volunteer Dates _____

Name of Organization _____

City, State _____

Type of Work _____

Volunteer Dates _____

TRANSFERABLE SKILLS

_____

_____

REFERENCES

Name _____

Organization _____

Job Title _____

Address _____

Email _____

Work Telephone Number _____

Cell Phone Number _____

How Long Known? _____

In What Capacity? _____

Résumé Worksheet continues

Name _____

Organization _____

Job Title _____

Address _____

Email _____

Work Telephone Number _____

Cell Phone Number _____

How Long Known? _____

In What Capacity? _____

Name _____

Organization _____

Job Title _____

Address _____

Email _____

Work Telephone Number _____

Cell Phone Number _____

How Long Known? _____

In What Capacity? _____

EXERCISE

RÉSUMÉ CHECKLIST: WHAT TO DO

☐ Include your name, address, phone number, and email address at the top.

☐ Select an appropriate format that includes a clean, professional appearance, and easy-to-read font.

☐ Make sure your résumé is brief, well organized, and focused on the position that you are applying for.

☐ Make sure it includes:

    ☐ Your education

    ☐ Any school activities that focus on your accomplishments

    ☐ Any relevant career preparation and training

    ☐ Your transferable skills

    ☐ Your past work history

    ☐ Statements that emphasize what you can do for the employer.

☐ Make sure your résumé is error free—no typographical, spelling, or grammatical errors.

EXERCISE

RÉSUMÉ CHECKLIST: WHAT NOT TO DO

☐ Do not include a date on your résumé; you should put the date on your cover letter (see the next chapter for more on cover letters).

☐ Do not include personal pronouns such as "I" in your résumé.

☐ Do not include abbreviations in the body of your résumé.

☐ Do not include personal information such as height, weight, social security number, driver's license number, race, religion, marital status, or political affiliation.

☐ Do not include miscellaneous details such as salary requirements, number of children you have or that are in your family, hobbies, or sports interests.

☐ Do not have typos (an automatic discard).

☐ Do not copy large amounts of wording from the job postings.

☐ Do not have an inappropriate email address like marienut@...mail.com, partyanimal@...mail.com, or cuteandlegal@...mail.com.

☐ Do not make it longer than two pages.

☐ Do not print on decorative or brightly colored paper.

CHAPTER THREE

Creating a Cover Letter

When you send a résumé to an employer via email, mail, or an online form, you must also include a cover letter. The cover letter is a one-page letter that you write to the employer expressing your interest in the job. It acts as an introduction to your résumé, explaining why you are applying for the job and how your strengths and skills match the position you are applying for. It should be typed in a business-letter format and proofread for spelling and grammar. It is unprofessional to send a résumé without a cover letter.

SOME THINGS TO REMEMBER

- Like a résumé, a cover letter is a formal document and needs to look professional.

- Your cover letter should be no longer than one page.

- It should be typed in a business-letter format, which contains the following information in this order:

  - your name and contact information

  - the date (including the month, day, and year)

  - the name and address of the person you are writing to

  - the greeting or salutation (example: "Dear …,")

  - the body of the letter (two short paragraphs—work experience/education/ skills)

  - the closing phrase (examples: "Sincerely" or "Thank you")

  - your signature

  - your typed full name.

SAMPLE COVER LETTER

Sarah Jones

1234 Hope Road, Towson, MD 23456

(301) 555-0101

sjones@gmail.com

January 7, 2017

Mr. Sam White

Sunshine Publishers, Inc.

101 Willow Drive, Nashville, TN 12345

Dear Mr. White,

I am writing to express my interest in the editorial assistant position at Sunshine Publishers.

I am a very detail-oriented person, which is important when fact-checking and editing manuscripts for grammatical errors. Grammar and the English language have always been a strong interest of mine, and I have excelled in related courses throughout my education. In addition to being detail-oriented, I am a hard worker and consider myself responsible and dependable. I am confident that I would be a valued employee at your publishing company.

I am interested in learning more about this position, as it seems like a great match for my skill set. I am enclosing a copy of my résumé for your consideration and am happy to provide you with references if necessary. Thank you for your time and consideration of my application.

Sincerely,

{Signature}

Sarah Jones

EXERCISE

COVER LETTER WORKSHEET

Your Name _____

Your Address _____

Your Phone Number _____

Your Email Address _____

Date _____

Name of Person You're Writing to _____

Their Address _____

_____

The Greeting or Salutation _____

The Body of the Letter _____

_____

_____

_____

_____

_____

_____

The Closing Phrase _____

_____

_____

Sincerely,

Your Signature _____

Your Typed Full Name _____

CHAPTER FOUR

Filling out an Application

Most employers will require you to complete an application. This is a document that will provide the company with some basic information about you, such as your name, where they can contact you, where you went to school, and other items. It is very important to fill the application out neatly and accurately. You can use your résumé as a guide as it will help you to remember important information such as your work history and references.

Sometimes you can go directly to an employer and pick up a paper application, but nowadays most applications are online. Whether you are filling out an application by hand or electronically, make sure that all information requested is factually and truthfully stated. Ask your teacher, advisor, career counselor, family, or friend for help if you do not understand something, and have someone proofread it for accuracy, content, spelling, and grammar. Then return the application as requested either in person, by mail, or via email.

ONLINE APPLICATIONS

You can find the company's job application using a Google search for their website. Once on the homepage, look carefully for the job link. It could be listed under a heading such as: Careers, Employment Opportunities, Job Opportunities, Join Our Team, Open Positions, Job Openings, or Work with Us.

Once you find the right page, carefully follow the instructions for application. Sometimes you may be able to type your answers into a website application and submit it right away. Sometimes you may have to download the application to your computer and fill it out by:

- printing the application (print two copies just in case!), filling it in by hand, and then mailing it, dropping it off to the employer, or scanning it back into your computer and submitting it as an attachment on the website or through email

- filling it in on the computer and submitting it as an attachment on the website or through email.

PAPER APPLICATIONS

Sometimes you have to obtain a paper application at the actual place of business you want to work, such as in a store or a restaurant. If so, make sure you are dressed in neat, clean clothes and that you have showered and combed your hair. You want to try to make a good first impression. Visit at a time when they are not busy. Some businesses prefer that you come in the morning before they get too occupied, while others would prefer for you to come at the end of the day. You can call an employer ahead of time to inquire about that.

When you walk into the place of business, find an employee and wait until they seem free to talk. Then walk up to them and say something like, "Excuse me, I would like to pick up a job application. Can you help me with this?" (Request two copies in case you make a mistake!) Make sure you say "thank you" before you leave with the blank applications. Fill it out later when you are in a place where you can concentrate and someone can proofread it for you. When you come back to drop off the completed application, the same rules apply: make sure you are clean and dressed well, deliver it at a time when they are not busy, and be polite.

CHAPTER FIVE

Going to an Interview

Interviews are a critical aspect of obtaining a job. Your résumé and portfolio may be of high quality, but the interview is where the employer gets an understanding of you personally. You must be prepared for your interview and then be able to project yourself in a calm, professional manner to give the potential employer the impression that you are competent for the job.

MOCK INTERVIEW

Ask a teacher, coach, or mentor to serve as a potential employer and role-play an interview for a job you want. Take the process seriously. When the interview is over, ask your mock interviewer for feedback on your answers and non-verbal behavior. You may even want to videotape the mock interview and watch the tape later with your job coach.

SOME QUESTIONS FOR YOUR MOCK INTERVIEW

- Did you look at our company website?
- Can you tell me about yourself?
- What are your educational qualifications?
- What past experience do you have?
- What qualifications do you have for this job?
- Do you think you can do this job?
- What is your greatest strength?
- What is your greatest weakness?
- How do you handle stress and pressure?
- Why did you leave your last job?
- How do you fit into this company?
- How do your skills match this job?
- What are your salary expectations?
- What do you enjoy doing?
- Why should I hire you rather than someone else?

- Which of your previous jobs did you enjoy the most and why?
- What do you consider one of your best accomplishments?
- Where would you like to be in five years?
- What are your goals for the future?

OTHER QUESTIONS THAT MAY BE ASKED

- Would you be willing to travel? Relocate?
- Would you be willing to work evenings or weekends?
- What motivates you?
- How would you describe yourself?
- How did you learn about our company?
- Why did you decide to interview for this job?

QUESTIONS YOU MIGHT WANT TO ASK DURING AN INTERVIEW

- What is the most important thing I need to know about this position?
- I noticed on your website that…
- What duties would be most important in this position?
- Will I be trained on the job?
- What is a typical day like on the job?
- Please describe a successful employee to me.
- What chances are there for advancement?
- How are employees supervised and evaluated?
- What salary and benefits are being offered? (Always ask this question last, unless the information is in the ad or on the website or offered by the interviewer.)

PREPARING FOR AN INTERVIEW

In addition to doing a mock interview, here are other ways to prepare:

- Find out as much as you can about the company you are interviewing with (I only hire people who have read our website). Remember to refer to it in your interview.

- Use a maps app on your cell phone or ask for directions to the interview. If you have time, go there the day before to make sure you know how to get there and where to park.

THE DAY OF THE INTERVIEW

- Dress according to the setting you will be working in. Make sure all clothing is ironed and free from wrinkles.

- Arrive 15 minutes early.

- Shut off your cell phone completely before entering the building!

- Greet the receptionist (in many cases the employer will ask them what they think of you).

- Bring several copies of your résumé and a separate list of references in case there are multiple interviewers.

- Bring your career portfolio and refer to the relevant sections during your interview.

- Ask for their business card before you leave (it is a good way to get the contact information of the person conducting the interview).

- At the end of the interview, thank the interviewer for the opportunity and say goodbye to the receptionist as you leave.

AFTER THE INTERVIEW

- Send a "thank you" note (this can also be an email).

  - You can add a comment about what you really enjoyed about the company.

  - Refer to something positive you talked about during the interview.

  - Tell them that you would really enjoy working at their company.

  - Tell them that you appreciated their time.

- If you haven't heard anything for a week, follow up with a phone call (only once) to see if they have made a decision.

DISCLOSURE

If you make it to the interview stage of a job application, you need to think about disclosure of your disability and when would be the appropriate time, if any, to disclose.

- Disclose before the interview if you need to:

  - request copies of interview questions

  - ask if the building is handicapped accessible.

- Disclose at the interview if you:

  - require accommodations to complete your job tasks, and need to discuss workplace accommodations with the employer.

- Disclose on the job if:

  - you want to discuss your disability after you start

  - you notice performance struggles related to your disability.

If you disclose after you start a position, you'll want to submit a disclosure letter to the Human Resources Department, and request a meeting with them to identify accommodations that would support you in completing your job tasks.

Search the internet for sample disclosure letters, reasonable accommodations, and for information regarding your legal rights under the Americans with Disabilities Act (ADA).

Sample websites:

- www.AskJan.org

- www.Autismspeaks.org (employment toolkit).

CHAPTER SIX

Preparing for a New Job

GETTING READY

There are several things you can do before starting a new job to make the transition much easier.

- Review your job description, employee manual, and any paperwork you have been given to understand the expectations at work.

- Start getting up earlier in the morning several days before you start so that you are used to the schedule.

- A day or two before you start work, do a practice run to see exactly how much time you need to get ready in the morning, how long it takes to get to work, where you will park, etc.

- Purchase a monthly bus or train pass or parking sticker if you need one.

KNOW THE DRESS CODE

Employers will often hand out a dress code, give you a uniform, require certain items for safety, or make general suggestions about what to wear:

- **A uniform:** If your employer hands you a uniform, be sure that you wear it every day, and that it is clean and wrinkle-free before you head to work. You may be required to wear a head-to-toe uniform, or just a shirt or hat. Make sure that the rest of your outfit complies with your employer's regulations as well.

- **Safety equipment:** Sometimes certain items are required for safety, like non-slip sneakers if you're a server at a restaurant, or safety goggles if you're working as a mechanic. Be aware of all of these and wear them when necessary.

- **Business casual:** This sounds confusing, but generally speaking, women should wear a skirt or dress with a hem past the knee, or tailored dress pants with a button-down or blouse. Men should wear dress pants or khakis, with a collared shirt and a belt. Imagine what your high school teachers wore.

- **Business formal:** Men should be in a suit and tie, and women should be in a tailored dress or pantsuit. Imagine what lawyers would wear in a courtroom, for example.

- **Casual dress:** This sounds like anything goes, but you should still be tasteful. Don't expose too much skin, especially on your stomach, chest, back, and behind. Avoid short shorts, tank tops, and see-through or worn-out clothing with holes, tears, or stains. Make sure your clothes are clean and wrinkle-free.

- **No dress code:** Even if your employer tells you there's no dress code, there's still a dress code. The same rules apply as for casual dress. If you're ever unsure, look around the office and wear clothes that resemble what your co-workers are wearing. And remember that personal hygiene is also important: you should always be showered, with your hair washed and combed, your teeth brushed, and your hands and fingernails clean.

THE NIGHT BEFORE YOUR FIRST DAY

- Make sure you have enough gas in your car, a bus or train pass, or enough money for the fare.

- Consider showering that night if that will help you be ready on time before you leave in the morning.

- Set your alarm early enough to accomplish all the tasks you need to do before work.

- Check the weather to see if you will need to add time.

- Set up your breakfast and pack your lunch.

- Organize your backpack with all the things you will need: a charged cell phone, keys, laptop, snack, pens, and anything else you need on the job.

YOUR FIRST WEEK ON THE JOB

First impressions are huge in your ultimate success.

- Introduce yourself to every employee you meet and remember to smile.

- Find out your schedule and any important meetings or dates and put them in your calendar.

- Find out when your supervision time is with your supervisor and put it in your calendar.

- Find out when and where they want you to take breaks, including lunch.

- Ask as many questions as you need to; be thorough, but don't overwhelm your boss.

- Make notes of critical information given to you about how the business operates, its goals, its deadlines, and how you fit in.

- Relax and appreciate the process; you will be spending a good portion of your life there, so enjoy it!

MENTORING

At some jobs you may request to have a mentor or role model to help train you in your position. A mentor is someone you can confer with to ask questions or get critical information on how to operate at your business; they agree to meet with you one-on-one and help you grow and develop on the job. An employer may provide time for this on your schedule.

If your company does not provide this service, then you can seek it yourself. Find a person at work who you can trust and who seems to know what they are doing—someone who has the skills you need to be successful on the job. Ask them if they could meet with you once a week to go over your job performance and answer any questions you may have. Ask them if they would be available for other questions during the week so that you can learn how to perform your job well.

If you have a supervisor who meets with you weekly or biweekly, you may not need to have a mentor and the supervisor may not want you to go to someone else for advice. Make sure you go through your supervisor first and then supplement with a mentor if need be. Don't quote your mentor or tell your supervisor what they've recommended, as it could become a problem if your supervisor thinks you are listening to the mentor instead of them.

EXERCISE

MENTORSHIP GOALS FORM

List the goals and skills you want to obtain on your job with the assistance of a mentor. Share this with the mentor at your first meeting:

A goal I want to achieve at work is: _____

A skill I need to have is: _____

A habit I need to develop is: _____

The training I need is: _____

The educational course I need is: _____

The changes I must make are: _____

SELF-REINFORCEMENT

No matter your job, some days at work, or maybe a part of every day, will be difficult. You may have to go through a long training day. Perhaps you have to spend a few hours, a week, or even a month on a project you really don't like. Or maybe it's inventory day at the store, which you find boring and almost unbearable.

In these cases, you can help yourself get through it by rewarding yourself for your hard work. For example, tell yourself that if you work hard all morning, you can get a hot chocolate at lunch. Schedule your day so that you can take breaks doing things you like—taking a walk, chatting with a friend, playing a game on your phone—but then get right back to work. (And only take breaks that your employer explicitly allows!) Finally, plan fun weekend activities and nights out with friends so that you have something to look forward to after your difficult day.

PITFALLS TO AVOID

While each career area will have its own challenges, there are a few common pitfalls to avoid on any job.

TOP TEN REASONS EMPLOYEES ARE FIRED

Some of the most common reasons employees are fired include the following:

- **Poor performance:** Make sure you know your job requirements and are fulfilling them to your utmost ability. If you find yourself struggling in a certain area, be proactive and ask your supervisor or mentor for advice.

- **Bringing personal problems into the workplace:** Leave your personal problems at the door.

- **Lying:** Be completely honest from the moment you begin filling out a job application. A lie can seem like a good solution at the time, but your employer will eventually find out, and your problems will multiply.

- **Missing work, being late, or taking unwarranted breaks:** Employers simply need their employees to be present in order for work to be done. If you are not present, you're not working towards the employer's goal, and you'll be let go.

- **Stealing:** Don't take anything, from a pen to a computer to someone else's idea.

- **Getting caught up in office politics or gossip:** Do not talk negatively about your co-workers or employer. When you're at work, try to keep the conversations productive and try your best to get along with everyone. If you're having trouble, refer to the "Teamwork" chapter of this book for help.

- **Complaining about work:** Whether it's at work, at home, or on social media, complaining about work will not solve anything, and your employer may find out. Instead, be proactive at work about solving the issues you find disagreeable.

- **Refusal to follow directions or orders:** Again, employers need employees to work towards carrying out the business's goal, and if you don't carry out your job requirements, you won't last long.

- **Unauthorized use of the Internet or email:** As we discussed in the "Technological Proficiency" chapter, spend your time doing work tasks only, and visiting only workplace-appropriate websites.

- **Alcohol or drug abuse:** Do not come to work intoxicated in any way. If you are having trouble controlling your alcohol consumption, visit a local AA meeting or see a substance abuse counselor. You will be proud that you took this first step to take care of yourself—and you will be more likely to keep your job.

COMMON BAD HABITS

Employers are often too reticent to tell you when your bad habits are causing problems, for you or for others. Instead, resentment builds, and in the end, you can be fired. Ask your employer periodically to give you an honest assessment.

AVOID THESE HABITS:

- **Poor planning:** Stay busy while on the clock. Don't, for example, spend your first hour at work wondering what you should work on that day. Instead, plan your next day before you leave work, and keep a list of tasks to work on when business is slow or your main work is done.

- **Procrastinating:** It is best to get unpleasant tasks out of the way immediately. If you wait, you will cause yourself and your co-workers undue stress.

- **Being late or unprepared:** Do your research before meetings or interviews, and arrive at all appointments, meetings, and conferences on time and with all required materials, such as documents, pen, paper, or laptop. If you arrive late or unprepared, it can cause problems for the whole day's schedule, and those who show up ready and on time can feel like their time is being wasted.

- **Putting personal life first during work hours:** Everyone has emergencies from time to time. But don't be late every morning because of something going on at home. Don't schedule appointments, like routine dental check-ups, during your own work hours. And don't overburden co-workers with personal information.

- **Responding slowly to emails or phone calls:** As much as you may not want to write an email or check your voicemail, communication is essential for workplace function. Your supervisor, especially, needs quick responses to his or her messages. And your co-workers and clients will quickly grow tired of your unresponsiveness.

- **Being loud or making irritating noises:** Keep your voice at the same level as those around you, and beware of making a noise by doing things like tapping your pen or swiveling your chair. Remember that others are around you trying to work, and that you may be disrupting them.

- **Poor hygiene:** A sloppy appearance will cause co-workers and clients to have a bad impression of you, even if you're the best person for the job. In addition to appearance, you should eat well and exercise so that you appear healthy and have more energy. Finally, clean up and wash your hands after using the kitchen or restroom.

- **Using inappropriate humor:** Be careful not to tell jokes that might offend your co-workers. If you're unsure, just stick to staying positive.

- **Not caring about your work:** Be enthusiastic about what you do, and do your best, whether you're stocking shelves or running the company. Everyone needs to have a realistic, positive attitude in order for the business to thrive.

STORY

One of our students, Lyle, got an apprenticeship at a local auto-part store. He had a certain number of tasks to complete each day, and once he completed them, he would sit down in the back room and stare down at the table, waiting for another task to come up. Even though Lyle was technically meeting all job requirements, his supervisor began to grow irritated seeing him sitting around while everyone else was working hard. Eventually, Lyle asked his boss for an honest assessment of his work performance, and the boss told him that he had to stay busy on the clock. He needed Lyle to be part of the team. Together, they came up with a list of secondary tasks Lyle could help with once he had finished his primary duties.

ATTITUDE ADJUSTMENT

There are three types of employees in the world:

- employees who have to be told what to do and then grudgingly do it

- employees who have to be told what to do and do it because they know it's right

- employees who are self-motivated and just do it!

Which one are you?

Probably the most common reason employees are fired is their poor attitude. Employers want employees who are eager to learn and grow and go with the flow. They don't want to have to convince their staff to work on projects. Your chances of success on any job are contingent on the relationships you develop with your supervisor and other employees. They don't all have to like you, but they do need to respect you and see you as a team player they can rely on.

Workability is the most crucial skill that you will need on the job. It means developing an attitude of willingness and openness towards learning new skills, trying new things, and working with all kinds of people. It means putting your ego on the shelf and working for the team goal.

STORY

Disrupting the work environment makes everyone uneasy. I always tell my employees at CIP to leave their personal problems at the door. I expect them to be available to our families and students and take care of their own business outside of work. At the same time, if an employee is having a major problem outside of work, I reach out and offer compassion or even assistance, depending on the nature of the problem.

Even if you have experienced several problems getting to work and someone in your personal life is being unkind to you, you cannot unload a tale of woe on other employees who are trying to get their work completed. One time at work I had to put up a sign that said "Drama-Free Zone" to deter a small group of employees from continuing to disrupt the emotional wellbeing of all. I also talked to each one individually to inform them of my expectations for them.

EXERCISE

ATTITUDE INVENTORY

Check the boxes that apply to you and then adjust your attitude.

NEGATIVE ATTITUDE

- [ ] Spread gossip at work
- [ ] Blame others for your problems
- [ ] Complain behind the scenes
- [ ] Ignore others' needs
- [ ] Act like you know everything
- [ ] Defensive about receiving feedback
- [ ] Promise things you don't deliver
- [ ] Procrastinate on work to be done

POSITIVE ATTITUDE

- [ ] Volunteer to help out
- [ ] Arrive on time
- [ ] Stay until work is complete
- [ ] Study how to improve outside of work
- [ ] Friendly to others
- [ ] Proactive in solving problems
- [ ] Ask for more work or training
- [ ] Encourage other employees
- [ ] Willingly accept help
- [ ] Accept new assignments willingly
- [ ] Say "thank you" to others
- [ ] Share your ideas freely
- [ ] Help without being asked

NETWORKING

At some point, you will probably want to move up in the workplace. You may want a raise, a better title, or more responsibility; you might want to run the company one day, or start your own company; you may need employees of your own; or you may want to be self-employed, working only for yourself on your own schedule. In all of these cases, you are going to need strong business connections and social networks to get to where you want to go.

It can sometimes be difficult for those on the Autism Spectrum or with Learning Differences to socialize at work. It often requires flexibility, spontaneity, and giving up some personal time. At CIP we always tell our students about "behavior at the water cooler." This means being able to make friends at work, even if it means making small talk at first about subjects you find uninteresting, like reality television or the weather. Your knowledge and intellect are important, but people also want to work with those they feel comfortable talking to. They want to get to know each other. The small talk can go a long way. Think of it as building your support system.

There are many benefits to expanding your social fabric. If there is an opening in your company that you'd like to have, your connections will help you advance. If your boss is irritated about something, a co-worker you've gotten to know may give you a heads up. The "water cooler" is where you will make friends and maybe even meet your spouse. If you leave for another company, or start your own, you can ask your former co-workers for advice. Be there for your co-workers, and they will be there for you.

STORY

Emma was an apprentice with a local electrician. Sometimes many of the people in the office and in the office next door would go out to lunch together. They always invited Emma to come along, but she always felt too shy. She liked to eat lunch at exactly noon every day, and she always brought her own lunch to work, which she didn't want to waste.

Emma's job coach came in to see how things were going, and she noticed that when her co-workers asked if she wanted to go to the bagel shop for lunch, Emma declined. The job coach told her that the soup she packed for lunch would still be good the next day, and that changing her schedule around a little bit was a small price to pay for the valuable connections she could make during casual lunches with her office mates.

Emma has since worked hard to be more spontaneous and flexible about slight changes to her schedule. This doesn't mean she has to go to lunch every day, but sometimes she does, especially if it's a special occasion. Recently, her co-workers all took her out to celebrate her birthday, and it felt good to be surrounded by co-workers who she knew cared about her. This couldn't have happened if she didn't take that first step.

You may feel shy about socializing. You may worry that you'll make a mistake, or say something offensive. If you are unsure, you can always say, "Have I said anything to offend you?" If you make a mistake, simply apologize. Be up front about who you are, and people will understand. The more you practice, the more comfortable you will be, the more you will learn, and the stronger your support system will be.

Conclusion

This workbook has given you the "tricks of the trade" for learning how to be proactive in finding employment and succeeding at work—but it is an ongoing process. Finding employment isn't always easy, but it is much easier than *staying* employed. Our goal is for you to be prepared for whatever changes happen at work or along the job search. The more you can understand and develop the personal and work habits described in this book, the more flexible and adaptable you will be when things need to change—and that means all the time! Even NBA teams have practices several times a week. They are constantly improving their skills, learning how to work as a team, and planning out plays and strategies that will work.

None of this can happen, though, unless you take care of yourself first, outside of work, so that when you enter the workplace, you can do your job without disruption. As someone who has been diagnosed with Learning Differences, I've spent the majority of my life learning how to better understand those differences and teach myself strategies to cope with them. I've learned that you need to become a self-change agent: to take action to organize yourself, handle stress, and take care of your sensory, social, and emotional issues. I've also learned that, although

no one can do that for you, there are plenty of people who are willing to assist you, at home, at school, or at work. *You must be willing to ask for help.* Without that, your success may be deeply limited.

The philosophy of CIP is that every individual is inherently valuable, and made for good purpose. By working your way through this book, we hope that you have not only learned the skills that will help you gain and retain employment, but also discovered who you are—gotten to know yourself, your interests, your goals, and your dreams. We hope that this will help you to pursue a career that not only supports you financially, but spiritually too.

"Your time on earth is limited, so use it wisely. Be in your own life fully and set your own path and follow it. Don't let the rigid thinking and dogma of other people override your dream. Be true to your vision and what you truly are; everything else is there to support you."

Michael McManmon

About the College Internship Program (CIP)

CIP's mission is to inspire independence and expand the foundation on which young adults on the Autism Spectrum, with ADHD and other Learning Differences, can build happy and productive lives.

CIP is one of the most comprehensive programs in the world for assisting young adults with learning differences to succeed in college, employment, and independent living.

- Founded in 1984 to help young adult ages 18-26 with learning differences make successful transitions from adolescence to young adulthood.

- The CIP program focuses on real-life skills in areas of social thinking, executive functioning, sensory processing, and wellness.

- Residential apartment living support prepares students for independent living.

- Each student's vision and goals are explored by a team of staff that dedicated to each student's personal success.

- Programs locations nationwide.

PROGRAMS & SERVICES

Full-Year Program
CIP's full-year postsecondary programs offer individualized college academic, social, career, and life skills support for young adults with Learning Differences. www.cipworldwide.org

Mploy Program
Mploy is designed for young adults with ASD and LD aged 18–26 who are interested in entering the workforce and transitioning to independent living. www.mploy.org

Summer@CIP
Experience independence and get a taste of college life at one of CIP's two-week summer programs on college campuses across the US. www.cipsummer.com

Endnotes

1 *Poor Richard's Almanack*, #651.
2 Letter to Robert Hooke, February 5, 1675, http://digitallibrary.hsp.org/index.php/Detail/Object/Show/object_id/9285
3 Speech, February 5, 2008, www.nytimes.com/2008/02/05/us/politics/05text-obama.html
4 "The Man in the Arena" Speech, April 23, 1910.
5 McManmon, M. (2012) *Made for Good Purpose*. London. Jessica Kingsley Publishers.
6 *The Death of the Moth and Other Essays*, 1974, San Diego, CA: Harcourt Brace Jovanovich, p.61.
7 *The Doctor's Dilemma*, 1909, www.gutenberg.org/files/5069/5069-h/5069-h.htm
8 https://hourofcode.com/us/promote/resources